PROCLAMATION:

**Aids for Interpreting the
Lessons of the Church Year**

EPIPHANY

SERIES B

**C. Fitzsimons Allison
and
Werner H. Kelber**

FORTRESS PRESS   Philadelphia, Pennsylvania

Library of Congress Catalog Card Number 74-24900

ISBN 0-8006-4072-1

Second printing 1976

5976G76   Printed in U.S.A.   1-4072

General Preface

Proclamation: Aids for Interpreting the Lessons of the Church Year is a series of twenty-six books designed to help clergymen carry out their preaching ministry. It offers exegetical interpretations of the lessons for each Sunday and many of the festivals of the church year, plus homiletical ideas and insights.

The basic thrust of the series is ecumenical. In recent years the Episcopal church, the Roman Catholic church, the United Church of Christ, the Christian Church (Disciples of Christ), the United Methodist Church, the Lutheran and Presbyterian churches, and also the Consultation on Church Union have adopted lectionaries that are based on a common three-year system of lessons for the Sundays and festivals of the church year. *Proclamation* grows out of this development, and authors have been chosen from all of these traditions. Some of the contributors are parish pastors; others are teachers, both of biblical interpretation and of homiletics. Ecumenical interchange has been encouraged by putting two persons from different traditions to work on a single volume, one with the primary responsibility for exegesis and the other for homiletical interpretation.

Despite the high percentage of agreement between the traditions, both in the festivals that are celebrated and the lessons that are appointed to be read on a given day, there are still areas of divergence. Frequently the authors of individual volumes have tried to take into account the various textual traditions, but in some cases this has proved to be impossible; in such cases we have felt constrained to limit the material to the Lutheran readings.

The preacher who is looking for "canned sermons" in these books will be disappointed. These books are one step removed from the pulpit: they explain what the lessons are saying and suggest ways of relating this biblical message to the contemporary situation. As such they are springboards for creative thought as well as for faithful proclamation of the word.

The authors of this *Epiphany—Series B* volume of *Proclamation* are C. FitzSimons Allison and Werner H. Kelber. Professor Allison, the homiletician, is a graduate of the University of the South (B.A.), Virginia Theological Seminary (B.D.), and Oxford University (D.Phil.). From 1956-67 he was Associate Professor of Church History, School of Theology, University of the South, Sewanee, Tenn. Since 1967 he has been

Professor of Church History, Virginia Theological Seminary, Alexandria, Va. He is the author of three books: *Fear, Love and Worship* (Seabury Press, 1962), *The Rise of Moralism: The Proclamation of the Gospel from Hooker to Baxter* (S.P.C.K. and Seabury Press, 1966), and *Guilt, Anger and God* (Seabury Press, 1972). He has lectured extensively at lay and clergy conferences, and in 1965 he served as the preacher on the Episcopal series of the Protestant Hour. Professor Kelber, the exegete, received his Ph.D. in 1970 from the University of Chicago. From 1970-73 he taught at the University of Dayton, Ohio. He is presently Assistant Professor of New Testament, Department of Religious Studies, Rice University, Houston, Texas. His study of the Gospel of Mark, *The Kingdom in Mark*, was published by Fortress Press in 1974.

Table of Contents

The Epiphany of Our Lord

Lutheran	Roman Catholic	Episcopal	Pres./UCC/Chr.	Methodist/COCU
Isa. 60:1-6	Isa. 60:1-6	Isa. 60:1-6	Isa. 60:1-6	Isa. 60:1-6
Eph. 3:2-12	Eph. 3:2-3a, 5-6	Eph. 3:1-12	Eph. 3:1-6	Eph. 3:1-12
Matt. 2:1-12	Matt. 2:1-12	Matt. 2:1-12	Matt. 2:1-12	Matt. 2:1-12

EXEGESIS

First Lesson: Isa. 60:1-6. This passage is part of the theology of Trito-Isaiah (chaps. 55-66), an anonymous author who reformulated the exilic message of Deutero-Isaiah (chaps. 40-55) for a postexilic situation. In 538 B.C. the Persian king Cyrus had issued an edict ordering the Babylonian Jews to return to their homeland and to rebuild the temple in Jerusalem (cf. Ezra 6:1-5). But this second exodus did not fully meet the high expectations aroused by Deutero-Isaiah (cf. 40:3-5, 9-11). The economic situation in the homeland was oppressive, and work on the temple was stalled by apathy and voices of discontent. Trito-Isaiah addresses himself to the exiles who have returned from Babylon to find their hopes frustrated by the realities of the Promised Land.

In Isa. 60:1-6 (which is properly concluded by v. 7) two major themes are developed: the epiphany of Yahweh and the pilgrimage of the nations. Generally, the two themes fall into vv. 1-3 and 4-6 (and 7). The imperative openings of each section are in the second person singular; the addressee is Zion-Jerusalem, home of the exiles. Jerusalem is to rise from hopelessness, because the coming of Yahweh will transform her into a place of light. The warlike features of older epiphanies (Judg. 5:4-5; Ps. 18:7-15) are absent; the focus is the light motif. Just as the sun rises in a blaze of fire, so will the epiphany of Yahweh fill Zion with light. With the rest of the world covered in darkness, Zion's magnetic force on the nations pulls them toward her light (v. 3). V. 4a, a literal adoption of Isa. 49:18a, introduces a description of the pilgrimage of the foreign nations. The five place names in vv. 6-7 indicate the universal nature of this journey to Jerusalem. Among the gifts delivered by the nations are first of all the sons and daughters of Israel (vv. 4b, 9b). The Jews of the dispersion will arrive in the company of the Gentiles (v. 4b literally reads: "your sons they bring them from far"). Other offerings by land and by sea are the nations' wealth and possessions (vv. 5-7).

Trito-Isaiah theologizes on a universal scale. Jerusalem's "covenant with death" (28:15) is canceled and the dispersing movement away from the

1

center will be reversed. All the Jews of the diaspora (not merely the Babylonian exiles), and "the full number of the Gentiles" (cf. Rom. 11:25) will enter into voluntary service for the kingdom of God. This is the promise of a new future for the returned exiles.

Second Lesson: Eph. 3:2-12. Ephesians is not so much a letter, i.e., a dispatch occasioned by the specific needs of a local church, as it is an epistle, i.e., a deliberate theological treatise dealing with the nature of the universal church. The author is a Paulinist, who, steeped in Paul's theology and writing under his name, at the same time moves beyond the thinking of his teacher. This epistle is often considered the most "ecumenical" of the NT documents, because its central theme is unity.

In Eph. 3:2-12 the author dwells on the mystery of Christ. The concept of mystery contains both hiddenness and revelation. The mystery had been hidden in God since creation (v. 9), and therefore removed from the grasp of all previous generations. It has now been revealed to Christian apostles and prophets. Although Paul is the least among these apostolic founders (v. 8), the mystery was also revealed to him at his conversion (v. 3 is probably a reference to the Damascus incident). The author conceives of apostles and prophets as the recipients of revelatory insights into the mystery of Christ. By implication, this sets them apart from Christians who learn of the mystery through the medium of the apostles' message. This "holiness" of the apostles is a subtle, but significant development beyond Paul, whose emphasis was more on the interdependence of all Christians (1 Corinthians 12), and less on the privileged role of one type of Christian. The mystery, most clearly spelled out in v. 6 and reminiscent of Rom. 11:25, concerns the participation of the Gentiles in the body of the church. The Gentiles' exclusion from "the commonwealth of Israel" (2:12) is to be corrected by their integration into the body. Jew and Gentile are to be joined together in the fullness of Christ who is embodied in the church. The Christian apostles are commissioned to proclaim that there is a divine plan operative in history to unite all in Christ.

This revelation of the mystery of unity defines the destiny of both man and the powers of the universe. The heavenly powers have separated man from God, depriving the former of access to the latter. This is the religious drama underlying v. 10. The church by its exemplary existence in unity will inform these heavenly powers of the collapse of the wall of separation. As a result, the unity achieves cosmic dimensions with Christ "filling all in all" (1:23).

Gospel: Matt. 2:1-12. The theme of the Matthean infancy narrative (chaps. 1 and 2) is the identity of Jesus: who is he and where does he come from? After his Davidic designation has been traced through the genealogy (1:1-17), and his name revealed by an angel (1:18-25), Matthew's story of the visit of the wise men designates the birthplace of Jesus.

Matt. 2:1-12 might properly be called a placement story, because it establishes Jesus' geographic origin. Bethlehem, disclosed at the outset (v. 1) and confirmed by the Jewish leaders (v. 5), is sanctioned by prophetic authority (v. 6). We encounter in v. 6 Matthew's practice of firmly anchoring all crucial aspects of Jesus in the Holy Scripture (cf. 1:23; 2:15, 18). Jesus takes the place of David in whose city he was born (cf. 1 Sam. 17:12, 15; 20:6). The formula quotation 2:6 is a composite, combining Mic. 5:2 with 2 Sam. 5:2b. From 2 Sam. 5:2b comes the statement that Jesus "will shepherd my people Israel." This supplement to the Bethlehem quotation proper carries additional weight. Born in David's city, Jesus is the royal shepherd sent to Israel, the people of God. The place determines his mission.

Despite Matthew's deliberate utilization of OT passages, his Jesus is not in all respects discernible as the fulfiller of Scripture. One should not lose sight of the fact that Matthew supports a Jesus who does not live up to the expectations of those in charge of Scripture. While the Matthean Jesus is indeed appointed Davidic shepherd over his people, his mission is primarily directed toward "the lost sheep of the house of Israel" (15:24; 10:6). Those physically handicapped, the women, and ultimately the Gentiles will make up the mixed community of this unorthodox Davidic shepherd. It is Jesus' unconventional fulfillment of Scripture which causes tension and in the end brings the cross.

This tension is already manifest in 2:1-12. The revelation of the place provokes a conflict between "Herod the king" and "all of Jerusalem" (v. 3) on the one hand, and the "king of the Jews" (v. 2) on the other. From the outset a counterstructure evolves in opposition to the structure of Jesus' life. His place is in danger. But Herod the Great holds no lasting power over Jesus. The wise men, even though appointed to wrongdoing, fail to become an instrument of evil. The wise men, representatives of the unusual and universal following of Jesus, find his place, worship the child, and return to their own land.

HOMILETICAL INTERPRETATION

Isaiah, Ephesians, and Matthew, here combined, focus the light of the Epiphany season with their respective themes. The prophet discloses the light to be wider than Israel and to include the Gentiles. Ephesians declares that the Gentiles "should be fellow heirs, and of the same body" and that this unity will disclose the eternal purpose of God. Matthew relates the fulfilling of this purpose in the visit of the wise men who have been drawn by the light of the star.

The modern wise men in W. H. Auden's "Christmas Oratorio" indicate how they, too, are drawn by that star "Onto that Glassy Mountain . . . where knowledge but increases vertigo . . ." The scientist, the historian, and the social scientist are led to exclaim respectively: "to discover how to be truthful now . . .," "to discover how to be living now," and "to discover how to be loving now . . .," and finally all together "to discover how to be human now is the reason we follow this star."

This modern adaptation of the Christmas story (by one of the greatest Christian poets of modern times) is an endless and unparalleled source of insight and wisdom. The issues of apologetics, secularism, ecumenicity, mission, and unity are particularly appropriate topics for Epiphany. Like ancient Israel the contemporary church needs continually to be reminded that it does not exist for itself. The mission of the church is an inescapable theme for the season and from the lessons.

"The church exists by mission as fire by burning" has been a motto of theologians of missions. In spite of growing cultural isolation and diminishing confidence within brand name denominations in Europe and the United States, the theological truths remain the same. As Johannes Blauw asserts: "The Church of Jesus Christ has the right, solely as a missionary Church, to call herself 'Church' at all."[1] The churches in the "third world" are showing the truth of this teaching as they manifest, especially in Africa, unprecedented vitality and growth.

Conventional idolatries of race, clan, and nation grow as cultural accretions on the hull of the ship of faith, thereby slowing its grace. They are scraped off as that ship endures the culture shock of crossing radical frontiers. The Light that is the light of the nations is hid by the encrustation of minutiae, inflated to irrelevant proportions, which are effective only in hiding the Light from those who are entrusted with its care but who are too timid and afraid to give it away. Hence, in the very action of the mission the church finds and refines itself anew.

The author of Ephesians knows himself to be the messenger of this mission, this new reality in Christ. The contemporary preacher, sharing with Paul the preaching entrusted to him, declares what had been unknown and now has been revealed. Ansolino in Hemingway's *For Whom the Bell Tolls* speaks of the darkness enclosing modern men: "We do not have God here anymore, neither his Son nor the Holy Ghost." Preaching the mystery is always needed everywhere. It not only passes across the boundaries of Israel and the world of the Gentiles but across the boundaries of the words of men. Even the principalities and powers in heavenly

---

1. *The Missionary Nature of the Church* (New York: McGraw Hill, 1962), p. 129.

places are informed by this new unity and community (=the ecumenical community, consisting of Jews and non-Jews) of the manifold wisdom of God (Eph. 3:10).

W. A. Visser't Hooft accurately pointed out that there was no theological justification for the plural of the word church. It is one faith, one baptism, one Lord, and one holy folk. We sing the words of "Onward Christian Soldiers" with little recognition of the scandal we are perpetrating by our continued unhappy divisions. "We are not divided, all one body we; one in hope and doctrine, one in charity." In the lessons, in theology, and in history the mission and the unity are one. As we declare the message, we participate in the mission, we become one in the common task, and the eternal purpose "purposed in Christ Jesus" is disclosed.

This exhilarating and promised purpose could lead the preacher, using the passage from Isaiah, to a very thorny but important issue. This third portion of Isaiah addresses itself to the exiles who have returned from Babylon to find their hopes frustrated by the realities of the Promised Land. The realities were in stark contrast to the vision given them by Deutero-Isaiah of their homeland and their new temple in Jerusalem. This discrepancy between the vision and the reality, between the ideal and the actual, between hope and history is among the most poignant agonies people always face.

One wise clergyman has observed that it takes a layman of unusually strong faith to survive the frustration and despair so often resulting from an inside knowledge of sin in the institutional church. Clergy themselves are often tempted to a subtle anti-clericalism, not knowing that a comparable situation exists in hospitals, universities, city halls, and business offices. Jobs, marriages, adulthood, and retirement have aspects that are like the Jews' disappointment on their return to Jerusalem when the Promised Land did not fit the hopes kindled in Babylon. In fact all life seems adumbrated by the hopes and frustrations of moving from Babylon to Jerusalem or from Egypt to the Promised Land.

F. W. Robertson preached one of his greatest sermons on this subject. It is entitled, "The Illusiveness of Life." [2] Two points are covered by the sections "The Deception of Life's Promise" and "The Meaning of That Deception." He points out that on one level the children of Israel were deceived by the promise of a "land flowing with milk and honey," that Abraham was deceived by the promise of inheriting the land. He, together with Isaac and Jacob, wandered in the land of promise "as in a *strange* country" and these "all in faith, not having received the promises . . ." (Heb. 11).

On another level, the meaning of that deception is that the promise is

2. F. W. Robertson, *Sermons*, 3rd series (London: Kegan Paul, 1886), pp. 77-89.

tailored to our present condition, while the subsequent disappointment causes us to look higher and live more deeply. Hebrews again shows that Abraham, Isaac, and Jacob dwelt in tents, as sojourners, because they sought a "city which hath foundations, whose builder and maker is God." Though they "died not having received the promises, but having seen them afar off . . . (they) were persuaded . . . that they were strangers and pilgrims on earth," knowing their homeland to be a heavenly one. The greatest disappointments seem to come with the greatest expectations. But in this case the meaning of the disappointment is not despair but a deeper and more mature vision. Robertson shows that God has no Canaan for his home, no milk and honey for animal appetites, "for the city which hath foundations is built in the soul of man. He in whom Godlike character dwells has all the universe for his own . . . 'All things,' saith the apostle, 'are yours; whether life or death, or things present or things to come; if ye be Christ's, then are ye Abraham's seed, and heirs according to the promise.' "

Nothing seems to remind us more of our condition as "strangers and pilgrims" on earth than our dreams. This present age especially needs to consider the part dreams play in Scripture. In this lesson from Matthew the wise men are "warned of God in a dream." In Genesis God came to Abimelech (20:3), Laban (31:10), Joseph (37:5), and Pharaoh (41:25) in dreams. In Numbers (12:6) God tells that he "will speak unto him in a dream." In Judges (7:15) Gideon heard of the dream of one of his men. In the NT the angel appeared unto Joseph in a dream and even Pilate's wife "suffered many things in a dream" because of Jesus.

Men's dreams are often unsettling and assumed by the age to be no more than autogenic. But in the light of these lessons the Epiphany season, and the example of Joseph and the wise men we may consider anew the unsettling aspect of dreams in the light of the "meaning of that deception," and as a means by which the gracious God "appears to" us.

The Baptism of Our Lord
The First Sunday after Epiphany

Lutheran	Roman Catholic	Episcopal	Pres./UCC/Chr.	Methodist/COCU
Isa. 42:1-7	Isa. 42:1-4, 6-7	Isa. 42:1-7	Isa. 61:1-4	Isa. 42:1-7
Acts 10:34-38	Acts 10:34-38	Acts 10:34-38	Acts 11:4-18	Acts 10:34-38
Mark 1:4-11	Mark 1:6b-11	Mark 1:7-11	Mark 1:4-11	Mark 1:4-11

EXEGESIS

First Lesson: Isa. 42:1-7. In the wake of the Babylonian conquest and destruction of Jerusalem in 587 B.C., the military and intellectual elite of the city was deported to Babylon on the Euphrates. Among the exiles was the author of chaps. 40-55 of Isaiah, generally referred to as Deutero-Isaiah. Speaking to a people who had lost home and political identity, he adapts the theology of Isaiah to the new condition of exile.

Isa. 42:1-9 is the first of the four so-called Servant Songs, all of which are found in Deutero-Isaiah (49:1-6; 50:4-11; 52:13—53:12). The protagonist of these poems is a mysterious Servant of Yahweh. Scholars have given him various identities: an unknown individual, the prophet Deutero-Isaiah himself, the king, or the people, collectively. At present many scholars prefer the collective identity (cf. Isa. 41:8). The language of the Songs is unmistakably messianic, e.g., much of what is said about the Servant could likewise have been said about the king. By the same token, the designation "Servant" was commonly applied to the king in ancient Near Eastern cultures.

Our first Song falls into two parts. The first part (vv. 1-4) depicts the Servant's official commission, and the second part (vv. 5-7 plus 8 and 9), a section formerly not part of this Song, outlines his universal mission. The speaker throughout is Yahweh, the God of creation (v. 5). In full possession of and guided by the Spirit of Yahweh, the Servant will impart justice to the nations (v. 1b). This propagation of justice is the most conspicuous assignment entrusted to him. Broadly speaking, justice (*mispat:* vv. 1b, 3b, 4a) indicates the divinely willed order of life which will prevail over disorder and chaos. The specific meaning of justice is spelled out in vv. 3 and 7. V. 3 does not speak of the suffering of the Servant, but of the Servant's compassion for the suffering people. Above all, justice entails an active concern for the oppressed. Through the assignment of the Servant the poor of the earth will recognize that their day has come. Quietly and without public fanfare the Servant will execute his mission (v. 2), which will produce nothing short of a covenant with the people of Israel and salvation for the nations (v. 6).

After the collapse of Israel's kingship Deutero-Isaiah reformulates salvation along the line of royal ideology. If one accepts the Servant's collective identity, it is the people themselves who will receive and implement the messianic promises.

Second Lesson: Acts 10:34-38. These verses form the opening words of Peter's sermon to the household of Cornelius in Caesarea. Peter is the dominant figure in the first half of Acts (chaps. 1-12), and Paul becomes the hero in the second part (chaps. 13-28). The career of both men is marked by frequent sermons, the famous speeches in Acts, which have been the object of scholarly debates. A generation ago it was argued that these speeches contain the pattern of the earliest Christian kerygma (C.H. Dodd, M. Dibelius), but recently they were identified as Lukan compositions (U. Wilckens). By and large, the speeches in Acts may well be understood as summaries of Lukan theology.

Peter's speech in Caesarea (10:34-43) appears in the context of the conversion of Cornelius (chap. 10). The latter is a watershed event because it signals the breakthrough toward the Gentiles; Cornelius is the first Gentile to be won for Christianity. Peter's speech tips the balance in favor of the Gentiles, resulting in the bestowal of the Spirit (10:44-45) and the Gentiles' baptism (10:47-48).

The introductory verses 34-35 appeal to the Gentile audience. The inclusion of the Gentiles is founded in the impartiality of God (v. 34). Fear of God and ethical conduct are the presuppositions for Christian membership (v. 35). Godfearers were Gentiles who sympathized with the Jewish religion, without fully submitting to its instructions. Cornelius himself had been such a Godfearer (10:22). The emphasis on doing good works is symptomatic of Lukan ethics (Luke 6:46-49; 19:11-27; Acts 20:35). V. 36 traces the origin and destiny of the gospel word. Originally intended for Israel, the gospel's limited appeal was transcended by its own object, Jesus the Lord. That Jesus is the Prince of Peace is a Lukan theme (Luke 2:14; 7:50; 9:54-55; 10:5; 19:38). Born in the year of the census and Zealotic violence, Jesus came to travel the way of peace (Luke 1:79). V. 37 traces the gospel's progress from John's baptism through Galilee to Judea. From there the gospel is to move through Samaria into the Gentile world and as far as Rome. V. 38 introduces the message proper of the gospel. The earthly Jesus, anointed at baptism, lived a life in Spirit and power; healings and exorcisms have confirmed God's presence with him. Peter preaches Jesus the benefactor whose ethical powers overcome the mortality of man. As such Jesus becomes a paradigm of Gentile existence in the world.

Gospel: Mark 1:4-11. Our passage is part of the Markan prologue (1:1-13). John, preparer of the way (1:1-3), announces and baptizes Jesus (1:4-11). Equipped with the Spirit in baptism, Jesus is driven by this Spirit into the confrontation with Satan (1:12-13). From this he emerges ready to embark upon his public career which opens with the proclamation of the gospel of the kingdom (1:14-15).

In the story of the appearance of John the Baptist (vv. 4-8) a desert tradition and a river tradition collide. According to v. 4 John operates in the wilderness, whereas in v. 5 he baptizes in the river Jordan. But "men do not go out to the wilderness to be baptized, but to the Jordan" (W. Marxsen). The phrase "in the wilderness" in v. 4 grows directly out of the preceding OT quotation of v. 3. John fulfills the precursor prophecy; he is the "one crying in the wilderness." Specifically, he is Elijah who was expected to herald the Day of the Lord (Mal. 4:5). His outward appearance (v. 6) is that of Elijah (cf. 2 Kings 1:8). His baptism constitutes an initiatory rite preparing the people for the gathering into the kingdom of God. John is the forerunner not merely in a temporal sense, but also paradigmatically. Although qualitatively different from Jesus (vv. 7-8), he is the model of what is to come. Causing a mass movement away from Jerusalem and out of Judea (v. 5), he anticipates the profoundly unsettling effects the irruption of the kingdom will have upon people. In the end, both John and Jesus will be "delivered up" (cf. 1:14 with 9:31 and 10:33).

The baptismal account (vv. 9-11) further explains Jesus' identity. The Son of God (1:1), whose identity is confirmed by the heavenly voice (v. 11), comes from Nazareth in Galilee (v. 9). In Mark's view Jesus is the Nazarene (1:9, 24; 10:47; 14:67; 16:6) who proclaims the kingdom in Galilee, dissociates himself from Jerusalem, and leads the way back to Galilee (14:28; 16:7). Mark does not report a Bethlehem tradition. His Jesus is from Galilee, not the fulfiller of the Bethlehem prophecy.

When Jesus rises from the water, he alone witnesses the heavens opened (v. 10). Accordingly, the heavenly voice addresses itself to Jesus personally (v. 11). The descent of the Spirit is not witnessed by John. It is an intimate affair between God and Jesus. From the moment of baptism Jesus is the Son of God, fully recognized, however, only by the Roman centurion (15:39).

HOMILETICAL INTERPRETATION

Whatever the identity of the "Servant" in these "Servant Passages" the preacher is certainly justified in applying them to the present ecclesia, the contemporary people of this covenant called to be "a light of the Gentiles." The expectation of the triumph of justice over disorder and chaos is proclaimed in Isaiah and something of its content is described as the prophet spells out what this justice means. To "fear God and to work righteousness" is the essence of Christian membership in the body according to this passage from Acts. The baptism of Christ indicates the fulfillment and personification of Isaiah's vision of justice and the personal content of the story related in Acts.

One of the themes that tie the lessons together is that of law-gospel. The justice of God that is the hope of Second Isaiah and the justice of God incarnate in Christ both lead to and through suffering to completion and fulfillment. The weight of this justice breaks all self-righteous attempts to carry it. The resulting suffering refines and expands the hope and the vision. In Acts, the boundary of Jewishness is broken by the weight of the *kerygma*, the story of God who is the God of all. The Gentile, like Cornelius, is included as the object of God's reconciling the world unto himself in Christ Jesus. This passage in the middle of the Book of Acts marks the transition from a local to a universal call.

It must be noticed that the weight of the law, the vision of justice, and the demand for righteousness are not diminished by Christ but heightened. The world knows, even better than conventional church people, the corrosive effects of religious and ethical demands. Theodore Reik, Sigmund Freud, Erich Fromm, and many other perceptive observers of human hurt have faulted Christianity because it makes too severe demands upon the self-esteem of an individual. It cannot be denied that Isaiah disclosed an even loftier vision of the people's vocation than what they had before inferred; and Jesus did not diminish the aescetic and prophetic demand of John the Baptist but moved it further into the center of men's hearts demanding more not less.

These times seem particularly eager to resolve the religious and cultural exactions by reducing their weight, lowering the demand, easing the obligation, and palliating the discrepancy between what we are and what we are to become. The world tells us that to have such a vision of righteousness by which we are judged, as that of Isaiah or especially that of Jesus Christ, is to enhance our guilt, lower our self-esteem, and trigger all the self-damaging dynamics of ill health. Better, they say, to lower the demands to realistic levels of human expectation which are, in some conceivable way, attainable.

Yet this unattainable and perfect vision is that shown in Isaiah ("He will not fail . . . till he sets judgment upon earth and we are called in righteousness"), preached in Acts ("Those who work righteousness are accepted by God"), and personified by Jesus as shown in Mark. What the world does not know is that a religion based on any "realistic" level of human expectation is a religion of self-righteousness. We are by the very impossible weight of God's law unable ever to have our dignity and identity based upon our self-righteousness. All self-righteous pretentions and idolatrous horizons are torn down and demolished by an honest and unflinching facing of the law. As the people of Israel are led through their history the narrow horizon of Yahweh as a tribal deity is wiped away. Especially here in Isaiah we see that the suffering endured in exile has produced wider dimensions of the original vision.

What the world does not know is that the unadulterated law leads to the gospel. As C. H. Dodd and others have taught: the law is a guard, guide, and schoolmaster that leads us to Christ. The weight of the law brings us to our knees, and we are now bereft of any self-righteousness that will fulfill the vision and empty of any arrogance that separates us from God's (and human) love. Sigmund Freud assumed the essential content of Christianity to be merely a lofty ideal (heightened super-ego material, in his terms) and people were already under more severe demands than they could fulfill from the ethical standards of a high civilization. He knew as Paul taught that "the strength of sin is the law" (1 Cor. 15:56). But he did not know the rest of the Pauline teaching: "For by grace you are saved by faith; and that not of yourselves: it is the gift of God: not of works, lest any man should boast" (Eph. 2:8-9).

It must be admitted, however, that much of what the world hears in the name of Christianity is merely law and it is quite understandable that a religion merely of law must be reduced to allow people breathing room. Hence, the new permissiveness increasingly pervades the world and the church. Those who fight such a trend only in the name of the law are unaware that such a strategy increases rather than prevents the lowering of the standards. After many years at the College of Preachers, listening to the sermons lay people heard from their clergy, Dr. Theodore Wedel reported sadly that too few had any *kerygmatic* context; the majority were an unrelieved recitation of the law's demands, whether personal or social in its dimension. One only has to consider what the word "preach" means to modern ears to realize how rarely the *kerygma*, which was preached in the early church and recorded in the Book of Acts, is being heard today. It is as though, with the domestication of the church, preaching is largely confined to Romans 12 ("I beseech you therefore brethren . . .") without opening up, unpacking, or explaining all that is implied in the "therefore." What Paul has shown in the preceding eleven chapters enables his listener to do what he exhorts in chapter 12. It is not enough for the preacher to be correct in his exhortation, he must also so declare the gospel that it enables the listener to do God's service.

The strategy then for the preacher is clear. The law in all its awesome demand for righteousness must not be lowered, nor adulterated, nor thought to be fulfilled by new idolatrous limits. Isaiah's vision of justice vanquishing over disorder and chaos, Acts' insistence that God is no respecter of persons but accepts all who work righteousness, and the fulfillment of both in the person Jesus baptized by John is not to be diminished, qualified, and tailored to fit the weaknesses, sins, and imperfections of a congregation. As impotent as the law is to enable sinners to fulfill it, the law is still "holy, just, and good" (Rom. 7:12). The effective preacher shows how the very inability to obey the law opens new horizons, as with Israel and the early church; purges arrogance, self-righteousness, and self-pity; and brings the hearers a wider hope, a nobler vision, and a deeper serenity in the gospel.

Tactics are always best left to the person on the scene. The strategy should in no way be so confining that the law must always be pushed to the point of the listeners' despair before the gospel is declared. George Whitefield realized this when he preached to Jonathan Edwards' congregation; skipping his usual prior use of law for conviction of sin, he moved immediately with that congregation into the good news of forgiveness. It might be that some today are unable even to hear the law until they first are made aware of the gospel foundation upon which the demand can be borne.

The Second Sunday after Epiphany

Lutheran	Roman Catholic	Episcopal	Pres./UCC/Chr.	Methodist/COCU
1 Sam. 3:1-10	1 Sam. 3:3b-10, 19	Isa. 3:1-10	1 Sam. 3:1-10	1 Sam. 3:1-10
1 Cor. 6:12-20	1 Cor. 6:13c-15a, 17-20	1 Cor. 6:13b-20	1 Cor. 6:12-20	1 Cor. 6:12-20
John 1:43-51	John 1:35-42	John 1:43-51	John 1:35-42	John 1:35-42

EXEGESIS

First Lesson: 1 Sam. 3:1-10. The First Book of Samuel presents a complex portrait of the man of Ramah: a Nazirite by virtue of his mother's vow (1:11), a judge (7:6, 15-17), a prophet (3:20), head of a guild of ecstatic prophets (19:20), priest (2:18; 7:9), and leader of the monarchic movement (10:1, 20-25; 16:1-13). This man of God served to unite the different religious interests of Israel. On a pilgrimage to the temple of Shiloh his mother Hannah, stricken with barrenness, had prayed to Yahweh for a son, and her prayer was heard (1:3-18). In fulfillment of a vow she entrusted Samuel, this son of prayer, to Eli, chief priest of the temple at Shiloh (1:21-28). Under Eli's supervision Samuel received training in the service of the priesthood (2:11, 18-20, 26; 3:1). The young priest's rise at Shiloh coincided with the decline of the house of Eli. The temple had been corrupted by the misconduct of Eli's sons (2:12-17), and Samuel himself is to pronounce Yahweh's judgment over the house of Eli (3:11-14). There is, however, no specific statement that Samuel was to be Eli's successor (1 Sam. 2:35 does not necessarily point to Samuel).

It was because of the priestly corruption at Shiloh that Yahweh had withheld revelations from the sanctuary (v. 1). The dimness of Eli's eyes (v. 2) is mentioned to explain Samuel's behavior. Samuel assumes that he is called to render service to a helpless Eli. The statement concerning the burning lamp (v. 3) indicates that night had not given way to dawn. The ark (v. 3) was the same cultic object which David transferred to Jerusalem (2 Sam. 6:12-19) and Solomon worshipped in his temple (2 Sam. 8:1-11). It was the throne of divine presence from which proceeded the call to Samuel. The threefold call of Yahweh (vv. 4-9) heightens the drama toward the climactic moment of revelation (v. 10). The divine presence is intimated in reserved language: "Yahweh came and stood" (v. 10).

1 Sam. 3:1-10 suggests that the temple is the traditional place of revelation. It was not unusual for priests to be prophets. Samuel "was established as a prophet of Yahweh" (v. 20) by perceiving the voice of Yahweh for the first time (cf. v. 7) and by delivering its message. Yahweh's revelation occurs by hearing, rather than in dreams or visions; it reaches Samuel awake. The revealed information is designed to make history (vv. 11-14).

Second Lesson: 1 Cor. 6:12-20. The Corinthian Christians drew drastic consequences from the Christ event. Christ, they believed, had saved them—no strings attached. As a result they were free and no longer subject to the conditions of the old world. Christ had rescued them from bodily captivity and historical confinement. Their speaking in tongues signified the language of the Spirit and the vocabulary of the new being. This is also why they engaged in sexual excesses. They confess Christ in a life of total freedom. They are believing Christians who act in good faith, and not immoral pagans who succumb to the titillations of the world. In 1 Cor. 6:12-20 Paul does not attack immorality as a lapse of virtue, but libertinism as a religious conviction.

"All things are lawful for me" (v. 12a) was the Corinthians' motto used to legitimize unlimited freedom in all matters, including sexuality. While in principle acknowledging the Corinthian freedom slogan (v. 12c), Paul qualifies the notion that salvation equals total freedom on seven points. First, the communal principle: "not all things are helpful" (v. 12b). Helpful (*sympheron*) is what benefits the communal whole. In Pauline ethics the profit of the individual is less important than the common good (cf. 1 Cor. 7:35; 10:33; 12:7). Second, the principle of constructive realism: "I

will not be enslaved by anything" (v. 12c). The uninhibited exercise of
freedom undercuts its very foundation, causing new forms of slavery.
Third, the eschatological principle: "God . . . will raise us up by his
power" (v. 14). The Corinthians live in spiritual intoxication and consider
the body the worthless part of man. For Paul man *is* body destined to be
resurrected. The eschaton makes its claim upon the present conduct of the
body. Fourth, the christological principle: "your bodies are members of
Christ" (v. 15). Membership in the body of Christ precludes intercourse
with prostitutes (vv. 15-17). Fifth, the anthropological principle: "the
immoral man sins against his own body" (v. 18). Licentiousness leads to
self-destruction. Sixth, the pneumatological principle: "your body is a
temple of the Holy Spirit" (v. 19). Both the community (3:16) and the
individual are the locus of the Spirit. Seventh, the soteriological principle: "you were bought with a price" (v. 20). Freedom is to be used in
responsible gratitude toward the Lord.

Paul rejects sexual libertinism. But he does so not by downgrading the
body and moralizing on the temptations of the flesh, but by restoring the
damaged reputation of the body.

Gospel: John 1:43-51. Presumably Jesus is still in Bethany beyond the
Jordan (1:28) when he decides to go to Galilee (v. 43a). After Andrew (v.
40) and Simon Peter (v. 41), Philip is the third disciple to be "found" by
Jesus. Philip in turn recruits Nathanael (v. 45). Cana in Galilee, Nathanael's
home town (21:2), is also the goal of Jesus' journey (2:1 ff.). Philip's
pronouncement that Jesus is "son of Joseph" (v. 45c; cf. 6:42) reflects the
Jewish custom of identifying a man by reference to his father. For Philip
Jesus' Nazarene origin is in fulfillment of the OT (v. 45b). But Nathanael
objects (v. 46a) with: "Nazareth! Can anything good come from there?"
This is the classic protest against the Galilean identity of the Messiah (cf.
7:52). The heart of the matter is the obscurity and unmessianic status of
Jesus' birthplace. Nazareth was an insignificant village in Lower Galilee; it
is never mentioned in the OT, the Talmud, the Midrash, or Josephus!
Nathanael's willingness to accept Philip's invitation earns him Jesus' praise
(v. 47). He is a symbol of Israel at her best, sincere and dedicated to God.
Jesus knows the character of Nathanael (cf. 10:14), and Nathanael expresses surprise at his knowledge (v. 48a). Jesus' reference to the fig tree
(v. 48b) assumes that he had "seen" Nathanael earlier under a fig tree
studying the Scripture in search for the truth. Overwhelmed by Jesus'
omniscience Nathanael confesses him as Son of God and King of Israel (v.
49). But Jesus discounts his confession (v. 50a). Faith based solely on the
miraculous is unacceptable. Greater things are promised (v. 50b), and Jesus
reveals himself enigmatically as Son of man.

V. 51, a notoriously difficult saying, is the first of a total of twelve Son of man occurrences in John. The traditional interpretation argues for the motif of unity: Jesus is the point of contact between heaven and earth (thus R. Bultmann, R. E. Brown, etc.). Recently W. Meeks interpreted v. 51 in terms of alienation and foreignness: Jesus is the stranger par excellence.

The Johannine structure of thought develops along a spiral path. Philip pronounces Jesus the Messiah of Nazareth. Nathanael reacts sceptically. Next comes Nathanael's confession of Jesus as Son of God and King of Israel. This in turn meets with Jesus' scepticism. Jesus is all that—and more. In touch with the heavenly world, he is the Son of man from above who has entered into the hostile world below.

HOMILETICAL INTERPRETATION

The call of Samuel and the call of Philip and Nathanael are contained in two of our lessons. Samuel is born into a time of the emptiness of revelation. The call of God had been withheld from the sanctuary due to the corruption in the house of Eli. When there is no call of God it is a barren time for any vocation; all occupations tend to be only jobs empty of meaning, of purpose, of joy. Perhaps Samuel's birth to Hannah in her barrenness is meant to be symbolic of the barrenness of a time when God's revelation is no more heard in the land.

Certainly modern times reflect this time of Eli when for much of the culture God is not only silent but dead. Harry McPherson, writing in the *Washington Post*, laments these times as having "many Indians but no chiefs." In all branches of the culture—in the armed forces, politics, arts, education, the church—there seems to be a paralysis of leadership. In Samuel's time this was due to corruption which had provoked God to withhold his revelation, his call. Samuel, himself a miracle from Hannah's barrenness, brings to his vocation both the prophetic and priestly strain.

This combination of priestly and cultic with prophetic and tribal perhaps accounts for Samuel's ambivalence toward kingship. Murray Newman's *The People of the Covenant* fills in for us the dire military and political threat the Philistines were to Israel in Samuel's time. One tradition found the monarchy quite congenial and kingship the answer to their present dilemma. The other tradition saw kingship from a more primitive perspective and thought that it would threaten the purity of covenant relationship with Yahweh. Although Samuel marks the end of the house of Eli he maintains the older traditions of Israel and combines them just in time to save Israel from devastation by the Philistines. The revelation comes to Samuel in the primitive and dramatic threefold call to the ear, the primary organ of the Elohist tradition. The call comes to Israel through Samuel who is the answer to Hannah's prayer to be delivered from her barrenness. Thus, the personal and social implications of the call are neither separated nor divided.

Amos warns of a famine, not a famine of bread and water but a "famine of hearing the words of the Lord" (Amos 8:11). It was such a time for Hannah and Israel. And it was prayer, arising out of the distress of this famine, that was answered by Samuel's birth. Then Yahweh gave not only Samuel to Hannah but also revelation and vocation to Israel. So today in our famine of "hearing the words of the Lord" the prayers of those distressed by their barrenness in job and life are given the call of God, "Follow me." These were the two simple words of Jesus to these disciples: "Follow me." All Christian disciples learn their vocation from these words. The traditional baptismal vow of Christians is to follow Jesus as Lord and Savior.

It is said that every preacher should have some diagnostic understanding of his times. Why now is there what Eugene Ionesco calls "metaphysical emptiness"? Why now this state that W. B. Yeats described as one in which "the best lack all conviction and the worst are full of passionate intensity"? St. Paul asks, "And how shall they preach except they be sent?" (Rom. 10:15), and then answers his own question: "So then faith cometh by hearing, and hearing by the word of God" (Rom. 10:17). The word of God came to Samuel by hearing. Why did it not come before? We are told it was because of the corruption in the house of Eli. Thus, the silence of God can be seen as his wrath.

The corruption in Corinth to which Paul addresses himself in this passage from 1 Corinthians has deeper roots than a mere lapse of virtue. It is not mere quaint metaphor that relates fornication and adultery throughout the OT to unfaithfulness and idolatry. Sex is often concerned with much more than sex: dignity, reassurance, revenge, identity, and meaning. The films by Fellini and Bergman vividly illustrate the religious dimension of sexual search. The OT is much more apt and relevant to our times than many suppose when it shows the crucial tension between a god of nature and the God of history, between the fertility cults and the worship of Yahweh. So much conventional understanding of Christianity sees sexual behavior as only a matter of character and morality. Actually Paul claims that sexual abberations and immorality are symptoms of much deeper religious distortions. In Rom. 1:19-32 he discloses the link between ceasing to worship God and the resulting sexual corruption. Some critics have suggested that Ingmar Bergman's trilogy, "Through a Glass Darkly," "Winter Night," and "Silence," is a commentary on this passage from Romans, which sees the loss of faith, fornication, incest, lesbianism, suicide, and god as a "creeping thing" as the judgment of God. William

Burroughs, in an article in *The Atlantic*, reports that his motive in writing about sexual depravity was to contribute to the growing body of literature that makes every conceivable corruption as explicit as possible thereby diminishing what can be felt as shameful. W. H. Auden prays for those who think "knowledge of the flesh can take the guilt of being born away" or that "simultaneous passions make one eternal chastity."[1]

The Corinthian situation to which Paul in this lesson addresses himself is a bit different from common pagan immorality. Although the Corinthian Christians doubtless retain a spillover from the notorious cultural reputation their city had earned as a capital of licentiousness in that part of the Empire, they are now Christians who are justifying such behavior on the grounds of "freedom." Our exegete has underlined the seven arguments that Paul marshals against this sexual antinomianism. Our contemporary situations certainly cry out for some sane and helpful word from the preacher in regard to similar conditions, and the preacher could do a lot worse than flesh out and illustrate the seven points Paul made.

One common theme must not be overlooked. Paul discloses a view, a way to see flesh and spirit and God that enables his hearers to be truly free. He knows that fussing at a fat man will not keep him from gluttony, neither will exhortation to purity keep people from immorality. Certainly the crucial matter to straighten out immediately is what Paul means by "flesh." The "carnal spirit" that seems common to the seventeen "works of the flesh" enumerated in Gal. 5:19-21 is a much wider and more subtle matter than anything connoted in the mind of modern man by the word "flesh." The denigration of the body, which is the reputed view of the Jansenist and the Puritan, is no effective antidote to sexual immorality. We can see in the example of the Corinthians that it was precisely this distorted and dishonorable attitude toward the body that provided the excuse for their licentiousness. If the body doesn't count and we are now really "spiritual," it doesn't matter what the body does. This view was perpetuated in church history by the Manichaeans who were often at the same time radically ascetic and licentious, whose "freedom" was deduced by just such a failure to honor and appreciate the holiness and dignity of the body.

True freedom in matters of service and morality is a result of response to God's call. "If you continue in my word, then are ye my disciples indeed; and ye shall know the truth and the truth shall make you free" (John 8:31-32). Like Philip and Nathanael all disciples will be free as they respond to his call, "Follow me," and that truth will make men free.

---

1. W. H. Auden, *Collected Works* (New York: Random House, 1945), p. 426.

The Third Sunday after Epiphany

Lutheran	Roman Catholic	Episcopal	Pres./UCC/Chr.	Methodist/COCU
Jon. 3:1-5, 10	Jon. 3:1-5, 10	Jon. 3:1-5, 10	Jon. 3:1-5, 10	Jon. 3:1-5, 10
1 Cor. 7:29-31	1 Cor. 7:29-31	1 Cor. 7:17-23	1 Cor. 7:29-31	1 Cor. 7:29-31
Mark 1:14-20	Mark 1:14-20	Mark 1:14-20	Mark 1:14-22	Mark 1:14-20

EXEGESIS

First Lesson: Jon. 3:1-5, 10. Unlike all other prophetic writings of the
OT, the Book of Jonah is not a collection of sayings by the prophet, but a
story about him. Jonah, the book's antihero, seeks to evade Yahweh's
command to change the wicked ways of the Assyrian capital Nineveh. He
flees on a ship, has himself thrown overboard in order to placate the
tempestuous sea, and is swallowed by a great fish. Three days later he is
vomited out upon dry land. After this experience Jonah carries out
Yahweh's command, and thus contributes to the rescue of the Ninevites.
Resentful of a God who is "slow to anger, and abounding in steadfast
love" (4:2), the prophet goes into a sullen retreat. But Yahweh demonstrates to him that his pity for Nineveh was justified.

Our passage (3:1-5, 10) reports Yahweh's renewed command after the
fish episode and Jonah's prophetic appearance at Nineveh. This time Jonah
promptly obeys Yahweh. That the message would be the same as before is
understood (3:4; 1:2). The description of the city reads: "Nineveh was a
great city to God" (v. 3b), i.e., in the eyes of God it represented the
Gentile nations. Jonah proceeds to the center of Nineveh (v. 4a) and
makes his proclamation of judgment. Nothing but the bare fact of the
coming disaster is announced. While Jonah is conscious only of retribution
(cf. 4:2), Yahweh is using the threat of judgment as motivation for
repentance. Vv. 6-9 narrate the fasting of the king of Nineveh, of his
people, and the animals. This massive repentance arouses the mercy of
Yahweh, and he decides to spare the city (v. 10).

The Book of Jonah is influenced by the universalist, humanistic ideas of
postexilic wisdom theology. Yahweh's mercy is not meant for Israel
exclusively. It can be granted to the people and even the animals (3:7;
4:11) of a hated foreign city (Nahum 3:1-7), if this city turns from
violence and corruption to Yahweh. Jonah represents the kind of particu-
larism that would restrict Yahweh's mercy to Israel. The God Jonah fears
is "the God of heaven, who made the sea and the dry land" (1:9); in
relation to other nations he is but the God of judgment. God tries to teach
Jonah that the presupposition of salvation is repentance, rather than

national origin. Jonah is truly a prophet of judgment, but he functions in the service of a God of universal mercy.

Second Lesson: 1 Cor. 7:29-31. In chap. 7 of 1 Corinthians Paul deals with the issues of marriage, divorce, and celibacy. He writes in response to questions asked by Corinthians (7:1), although the theological stance of these Christians is not fully clear. It is widely assumed that Paul encounters two basic trends in Corinth: the libertinists who consider unlimited sexual freedom a sign of salvation (1 Cor. 5:1-2; 6:12-20), and an ascetically inclined group which regards sexual intercourse as sinful. This latter group possibly influenced Paul's writing of chap. 7. Ultimately, both directions express contempt for the body and discredit it as a creation of God.

Despite certain ascetic leanings on the part of Paul himself, the purpose of chap. 7 is not to recommend asceticism as a way of life, but to define the freedom of the individual (vv. 7, 17, 24) in a passing world. Salvation does not require a change in social status (v. 20), because no position is endowed with more grace than another (v. 7b). Therefore the unmarried should stay single, although this should not be made a rule either (vv. 8-9). Likewise, the married ought not to seek separation (vv. 10-11, 27a), although divorce is not unthinkable (v. 11a), despite the Lord's prohibition (v. 10).

The eschatological argument begins with v. 26. The "impending distress" indicates the anxiety of the end time. In the last analysis, it is for apocalyptic reasons that the *status quo* is to be maintained. Those who now choose marriage will get themselves most severely entangled in the crisis of the world (v. 28). Vv. 29-31 sum up the nature of Christian life under the force of eschatology. Because time is foreshortened (v. 29a) the believer is no longer to involve himself in the structure and struggle of the old world. Detached from all earthly conditions, he is to live "as if not," because "this world in its basic structure is (already) in the process of perishing" (v. 31b). In themselves vv. 29-31 could have been spoken by a Stoic, and yet Paul does not counsel withdrawal from the world into the inner self, but perseverance in one's place. Nor does he recommend abstinence from worldly goods because such are evil. The goods are relativized, but not debased. In the literal sense, Pauline ethics is time-conditioned. Under the pressure of the end time, Paul discovers the transience of all goods. *Sub specie aeternitatis* everything loses its earthly glamor. No change is needed, for total change is expected.

Gospel: Mark 1:14-20. The Jesus of "Nazareth in Galilee" (1:9) emerges from his wilderness confrontation (1:12-13) and enters Galilee to make it the place of his first public proclamation (1:14-15). His arrival follows on the heels of John's exit. The Galilean manifesto is called "the gospel of God," and its major concern is "the kingdom of God" (v. 15a). The principal identity of the Markan Jesus is that of proclaimer and bearer of the kingdom. All aspects of his career must be viewed in light of his programmatic kingdom announcement. The latter is divided into kergyma (v. 15a) and parenesis (v. 15b). Scholarly opinions differ with regard to the status of the kingdom: has it actually arrived, or is it merely at hand? Most interpreters opt for the nearness of the kingdom, but the eschatological force of the kerygma is such that arrival and presence could well be the meaning of Jesus' gospel. Repentance and faith, the parenesis, do not necessarily constitute acts of preparation for the kingdom. Rather they might indicate the direct consequences ensuing from the arrival of the kingdom. A radical break with one's former mode of living and confidence in view of the eschatological happening—these are the demands imposed upon people who live in the wake of the irruption of the kingdom.

Immediately following the announcement of the kingdom the evangelist reports the enlistment of four men into the service of discipleship (1:16-20). Discipleship is one of the pivotal topics in Mark. If it is the kingdom which is of concern to the Markan Jesus, then the call of the disciples accords it a communal dimension. The kingdom consists of people, but in the curious sense of dislodging them from their native habitat. Following Jesus requires a break with past life. But discipleship is not an end in itself. Jesus' call: "I will make you to become fishers of men" (v. 17b) entails a program which points to the future. Throughout his ministry Jesus will instruct the disciples with the aim of making them fishers of men. Primarily through exorcisms, healings, and teaching (6:7, 13, 30) are they to continue the legacy of Jesus. The gospel's reader who learns of the vocation of these men looks upon them as the founding figures of the kingdom. In their vocation he recognizes his own origin and vocation. He can follow Jesus if he continues the work in and for the kingdom of God on earth.

HOMILETICAL INTERPRETATION

Among the themes contained in these lessons is the continuing Epiphany theme of the worldwide mission of the church. Jonah's resistance to the mission and God's disclosure of his universal claim and love dramatize this theme. The short passage from Corinthians gives us a look at all present life through the perspective of the end and imminent judgment. Mark tells of the proclamation of the kingdom and its relation to repentance, belief, and the calling of the disciples. If one focuses on the theme of repentance it is important to undergird the common assumption concerning the chronology of repentance and forgiveness with some vehicle of grace that enables repentance.

In Jonah it is judgment. The judgment of Yahweh pursues Jonah on the sea and in the fish until he consents to preach this judgment to Nineveh. The judgment breaks the bondage of Jonah's idolatrous fixation on what he insists are the limits of Yahweh's grace and thus enables Jonah to repent and to preach. The judgment he proclaims against the city evokes repentance by the people, fasting by all from king to beasts, and repentance even of Yahweh, who changes his mind and spares the city. It is an awkward theme for tidy minds to have almighty God repent. It seems to involve the most primitive aspects of anthropomorphism. However, what is said of democracy can be said even more aptly of anthropomorphic symbols of God: "Democracy is the worst form of government, except for all the alternatives." So all the alternatives to human analogies for God are worse than the human ones. That God is some "force," "primal cause," or "creating principle" contains far more reductionist and dehumanizing connotations than "Father." In both Old and New Testaments we have portraits of God whose will and action are changed by prayer and repentance. Charles Simeon's response to the charge of being unsystematic in presenting God's treatment of men and salvation was that he "refused to be more systematic than the scripture." It is a good rule for preachers of any day.

The repentance in Mark's account also comes after judgment and even before "belief" (1:13). But here the content of judgment is the kingdom of God. "The time is fulfilled and the kingdom of God is at hand." This judgment becomes the occasion and leverage for repentance and belief. There is strong psychological evidence that people cannot repent by mere exercise of their wills. There must be some judgment, some tragedy, some dying, some new hopes, or some word that makes it possible for one to repent, to have one's mind changed. In the Episcopal *Book of Common Prayer* there is profound wisdom in the absolutions in Morning and Evening Prayer that include petitions to be granted "true repentance" after the declaration of absolution. Provision is made here for the ambiguity in human wills known to every perceptive pastor. Forgiveness and mercy are inaccessible without repentance but the truest repentance is the grateful response to forgiveness and mercy. Hence, as Christians our lives are characterized by the symbiotic and mutual relationship between repentance and forgiveness. The prodigal son's repentance was not finished, but begun, in the pig-pen. One characteristic common to all saints is their deepening repentance as their sense of God's mercies widens.

Regardless of the differences among scholars concerning the emphasis upon the "realized" kingdom, the preacher should be confident that it is eminent, immanent, and imminent. Any emphasis on one that excludes the others is false to the data and to the experience of the faithful. The kingdom is eminent: it is higher, loftier, and of greater priority than any other allegiance. Its claim is first, over that of nation, church, parents, spouse, or job. Thus, the kingdom always comes in judgment on lesser priorities and even duties and obligations. The hard saying about being not worthy of the kingdom without "leaving" or even "hating" all lesser claims illustrates the absolute demand of the eminence of the kingdom. Even Israel (e.g., Jonah's experience) cannot see itself as coterminous with the kingdom. The attempt to equate the church with the kingdom is to forget the lesson of Jonah and to create a new idolatry that reduces all prophetic self-criticism of the church to disloyalty. The eminence of the kingdom brooks no higher loyalties and no fidelity to any lesser end is finally acceptable. The eminent kingdom is the test of idolatry.

The immanence of the kingdom on the other hand is realized already. Wherever demons are cast out and people healed in the name of Christ the kingdom "has come upon you." The other side to the denial that Israel or the church can be equated with the kingdom is that they cannot be separated either. Although the kingdom of God is always judging the holy folk, the church is the indwelling locus of the kingdom in history. After hearing a long lecture by a young historian cataloguing distortions and faithlessness of the church, A. T. Mollegen, when asked what he thought, replied, "But the lecturer forgets that it is the only church we have." However inadequate the people of Israel were, it was the only Israel we had. There is a certain subtle arrogance in being so critical of the church in one's vision of purity and perfection that it becomes a barrier to the commitment, loyalty, and love of the church in history. The immanent kingdom is inevitably involved in institutions "far gone from original righteousness" and any individual whose dignity is too pure to be compromised by the ambiguities in the church, already possesses a purity "too good for this world" but does not belong to the eminent kingdom either. The immanent kingdom is the test of humility and courage.

The imminent kingdom shares attributes of the other two aspects but brings the final eschatological judgment to bear on each moment of history. The hard sayings mentioned above and the passage of Paul in Corinthians can only be seen gracefully in the perspective of the imminent kingdom. Because history is in the hands of God, and no one knows the "hour when the bridegroom cometh," we must all live now aided by the perspective of the end. This view helps hinge our hearts and wills to the solid foundation of the kingdom by which we can swing through all threats, tragedies, and suffering. The imminent kingdom is the last word. This is reassuring in tragedy but disconcerting to self-righteousness. Has anyone ever said (or felt), "If it's the last thing I ever do, I'll get revenge!"? If so, it is a prayer for hell. We have seen the last word in Christ. "Vengeance is mine saith the Lord." The demands of the imminent kingdom dig their foundations deeper than our marriages, families, and nations. "Meats for the belly, and the belly for meats: but God shall destroy both it and them," Paul declares in 1 Corinthians 6. In our passage from chap. 7 he is not speaking of the immanent kingdom but he is speaking of the imminent kingdom that prepares us for inevitable loss and gives us the final perspective by which to look at such good things as sex and marriage, "for the fashion of this world passeth away." The imminent kingdom is the test of the ultimate commitment.

". . . and they left their father Zebedee in the ship . . ." This poignant remark points to one of the costs of discipleship, the imminent and eminent dimensions of the kingdom place all other relationships and duties in subordinate positions. That this cost is no stoic ideal but good news, even "an easy yoke," needs to be proclaimed as desperately as any aspect of the gospel. C. S. Lewis's treatment of *storge*, the domestic and filial affections and loyalties appropriate in a family, is a superb help in showing how a good thing (domestic loyalty) can be bad.[1] It is from the demonic aspects of *storge* that we are rescued by *agape*. So much conventional Christianity is understood to be no more than domestication. This end of harnessing all drives and aims to the family is a source of much unnecessary strife and misunderstanding. The simple but subtle point, that because something is good it does not mean it is good enough, needs to be made. The total demand of the kingdom and *agape* sets us free from trying to reduce redemption to mere domestic harmony. The latter is a by-product of the total and mutual commitment to that Family that transcends the limitations of all earthly families.

The Fourth Sunday after Epiphany

Lutheran	*Roman Catholic*	*Episcopal*	*Pres./UCC/Chr.*	*Methodist/COCU*
Deut. 18:15-20	Deut. 18:15-20	Deut. 18:15-20	Deut. 18:15-22	Deut. 18:15-22
1 Cor. 8:1-13	1 Cor. 7:32-35	1 Cor. 8:1b-13	1 Cor. 7:32-35	1 Cor. 7:32-35
Mark 1:21-28	Mark 1:21-28	Mark 1:21-28	Mark 1:21-28	Mark 1:21-28

EXEGESIS

First Lesson: Deut. 18:15-20. The Book of Deuteronomy is not solely a legal code, but rather a mixture of laws, parenesis, covenant obligations,

1. C. S. Lewis, *The Four Loves* (New York: Harcourt Brace, 1960).

blessings and curses, as well as promises. In its final version the book presents "a compendium and summary of the whole law and wisdom of the people of Israel" (Luther). Deuteronomy is often linked up with the reform movement undertaken by King Josiah (640-609 B.C.) in Judah (cf. 2 Kings 22-23). Although the document may in some measure have been instrumental in Josiah's reforms, large parts of it appear to be of northern origin. It is safe to say, however, that the Deuteronomist, the final redactor of the individual units of material, addressed his theology to the Israel of the monarchic period.

While speaking to the people of the seventh century, Deuteronomy purports to be a speech of Moses. It is presented in the guise of Moses' farewell speech delivered in Moab forty years after the exodus and before entering the Promised Land (1:1-5). By redacting older traditions, the Deuteronomist uses Moses, figure of the distant past, as Yahweh's mouthpiece to discuss the issues of a people who are centuries removed from exodus and occupation.

Deut. 18:15-20 is situated in the broader context of a thematic treatment of prophecy (18:9-22). Following a prohibition of all forms of divination and sorcery (vv. 9-14), a prophet like Moses is announced who is to replace the perverters of prophecy (vv. 15-20); a criterion is added which serves to discriminate between true and false prophets (vv. 21-22).

The promised prophet (vv. 15, 18) will mediate between Yahweh and the people in the manner and power of Moses. In lieu of a specific ordinance from Yahweh, the Deuteronomist resorts to a scriptural argument (vv. 16-18). The old Sinai tradition reveals Israel's wish to be spared the immediacy of Yahweh's presence (Deut. 5:22-27). Yahweh honored this request by instituting the role of mediating prophet. This prophetic institution is not necessarily to be understood as a futuristic, messianic promise. It could just as well have served to confirm the office of the prophet for Israel. The passage explains how Yahweh through Moses provided for the institution of prophecy. Yahweh anticipated and sanctioned the existence of prophecy in Israel. The integrity of the office requires the people's obedience (v. 19) as well as the prophet's loyalty to Yahweh (v. 20). Both Qumran and early Christians, recognizing the futuristic proclivity of Deut. 18:15-20, interpreted the prophetic promise messianically (cf. 4 Q Testimonia 5-8; Acts 3:22-23; 7:37).

Second Lesson: 1 Cor. 8:1-13. The issue of "food offered to idols" (v. 1a) transports us into the Hellenistic world of mystery cults and sacrificial rites. Many religious ceremonies involved animal sacrifices. Part of the meat was burnt on the altar, and part of it was either sold on the market or offered at banquets. By and large the Corinthians had no scruples about eating this latter meat. Paul reveals the theoretical basis of their practice in vv. 1 and 4; in each case the clause "we know that" introduces a religious confession current at Corinth. "All of us possess knowledge" entails the conviction that "there is no God but one," for which reason "an idol has no real existence." The radical application of monotheism produces a sense of superior knowledge which shatters the Hellenistic universe of gods. The issue of eating meat sacrificed to a god is thus rendered obsolete.

Paul rejects the Corinthians' enlightened disavowal of the existence of gods (v. 5). Supernatural powers do indeed exist (as for Pauline demonology, cf. 10:19-22). But for the believer in God the creator and Jesus Christ the mediator of creation (v. 6) these gods have lost all power over man. They can still be effective, however, for people who do not possess full knowledge yet (v. 7a). If knowledge of salvation results in slighting these "weaker" people, it is deficient and lacking in perception (v. 2). Granted the iconoclastic force of the Christ event (v. 8), the newly acquired knowledge ought not to be made a rule and used against people. This type of knowledge "puffs up" (v. 1b), i.e., it becomes an end in itself at the expense of those who do not fully know. "Love" is the Pauline corrective against the Corinthian theology of superior knowledge and unadulterated freedom (cf. chap. 13). The essence of love is the "upbuilding" (v. 1b) of, or concern for, the weaker brother. Out of consideration for people who still have strong feelings about sacrificial meat, all should abstain (vv. 7-13). For if one's outlook is still dominated by belief in gods, the eating of meat offered to gods will breed feelings of guilt and anxiety. What is freedom for some might thus be the cause of bondage for others.

Pauline ethics does not imply the carrying out of a principle for the sake of consistency. Rather it suggests concession to the weaker ones, even if they do not act in full faith.

Gospel: Mark 1:21-28. Jesus' first public action after the calling of the four disciples (1:16-20) is an exorcism. As he enters the synagogue of Capernaum, he finds himself engaged in a confrontation with hostile forces. The overriding motif of Mark 1:21-28 is a power struggle.

At the outset Jesus' teaching is strongly emphasized (vv. 21-22; cf. v. 27). Although its content is not articulated, it is characterized as a teaching in authority (v. 22b), in opposition to scribal expertise (v. 22b), and of absolute novelty (v. 27c). Resting on the power and commission of God, Jesus' message spells out a radical alternative to the present ordering of life. This new set of priorities which Jesus introduces at Capernaum is inseparable from his programmatic kingdom message (1:14-15). It is by means of teaching and exorcising (as well as healing) that he institutes the rule of God on earth.

Provoked by Jesus' words of authority a man possessed by an unclean spirit screams aloud: "Have you come to destroy us?" (v. 24c). The evil spirit properly recognizes the power and purpose of Jesus' mission. Jesus is both the man from Nazareth (v. 24b) and the Holy One of God (v. 24d) who came to overthrow not merely a single proponent of evil, but the demonic power structure itself. In response to the spirit's pained confession Jesus "rebukes" him (v. 25a). The rendering of *epitimao* with "rebuke" or "reproach" is, however, inadequate. This verb, a technical term in exorcism language, connotes an aggressive act to wrest the power away from an opponent (cf. 8:32-33). Jesus divests the evil spirit of his authority and deprives him of his base of power (v. 25). The defeat of the spirit is signalled by the man's convulsion and a loud cry at the moment of exit (v. 26). The audience is perplexed and yet senses the eschatological dimension of the event (v. 27). Jesus' fame spreads throughout Galilee (v. 28).

Jesus' exorcism at Capernaum causes a clash between the kingdom of God and the kingdom of Satan. Fundamental to the event is the struggle of two kingdoms. By the power of his new word Jesus challenges a conventional order of life and crushes the powers of darkness. Out of the confrontation with Satan's subordinate, the unclean spirit, God's kingdom becomes a reality on earth. In the process of this power struggle Jesus' identity is revealed—out of the mouth of the enemy. It is the Spirit-filled Son who overcomes the evil spirit.

HOMILETICAL INTERPRETATION

The material in Deuteronomy promising a prophet follows, and is in contrast to, the castigation of all forms of witchcraft and divination. The Second Lesson is Paul's advice concerning eating meat sacrificed to idols. It contains his assumption that although the idols are nothing, supernatural powers of evil do exist. Mark launches Jesus' ministry almost immediately with an exorcism of an unclean spirit. It has been difficult for modern minds to grasp biblical assumptions concerning the sinister existence of evil forces. Histories of witchcraft abound with such phrases as "until the end of the 17th century" referring to some practices of magic and superstition practiced in the West. Those of us who are the products of the 18th century Enlightenment, 19th century industry, and 20th century technology have perhaps only recently begun to take seriously the weird things that have been largely banished to the edge of civilized man's consciousness.

Joseph Addison's famous hymn "The Spacious Firmament on High" (1712), based on Psalm 19, is a beautiful example of high confidence in the basically rational nature of the universe. This remarkable, and historically unique, confidence is at least partially the product of the revelation of God the *Logos*. The early church reinterpreted the Deuteronomic prophecy to mean Christ, the superstition banishing "Lord of Creation," and passed this confidence in regard to nature on to Addison so that indeed this prophet did historically banish, if not obliterate, the sorcery, divination, and witchcraft that had survived so many centuries in Christendom. Addison's faith, and that faith alone, enabled him to write:

> In reason's ear they all rejoice
> And utter forth a glorious voice;
> For ever singing as they shine,
> "The hand that made us is divine." [1]

We did, however, pay an expensive price for that confident assumption of the essential rationality of man and nature that characterized so much, if not all, of the eighteenth century. The price was a deism that ceased to ask the questions to which revelation is an answer and left us unprepared for the irrational aspects of both man and nature. The contemporary preacher is facing a situation somewhat new for western culture in the revival of sorcery, divination, witchcraft, and other "abominations to the Lord" that the prophet was to replace in Deuteronomy. It has come as something of a surprise to some to discover, as one clergyman put it, "All the spirits ain't the Holy Spirit." Discernment of spirits is one of the much needed gifts.

Jesus' discernment and exorcism of the unclean spirit provide some guidelines for a sermon focused on this issue. On the one hand, to ignore or deny a realm of unseen spirits, good and evil, is to be unbiblical and to make the eighteenth century mistake all over again. On the other hand, to relinquish the *Logos*-given skepticism toward superstition or the confidence in the Holy Spirit as that by which we can make sense of nature and human nature is to slip back into the weird world of superstition, darkness, and death. The promise made in Deuteronomy to raise up a prophet for us is finally completed in Christ.

The theological arguments concerning the *filioque* clause are complex indeed but one of the quite practical points in favor of the clause is that we discern the spirits by the Christ. It is he by whom the spirits are measured. The two natures of Christ could be helpful guidelines in the preacher's approach to the apparently accelerating growth and influence of exotic sects and strange groups. The fullness of his humanity condemns any solution to the problem of being human that destroys anything human. "Grace never destroys nature." Redemption is not destruction but a fulfillment. The fullness of his divinity saves us from any self-help, self-righteous religious solutions. This was no hero who tried harder, who

1. *The Hymnal* (New York: Oxford University Press, 1940), no. 309.

was a more clever scribe, who had insights "before his time." This was "God in Christ reconciling the world unto himself." God who is invisible is known by the "express image of his person." By Christ we not only know what it means to be truly human, but also what kind of God we have.

The issue of meat offered to idols in the Corinthian selection would seem at first glance to be an obsolete question. Few congregations in the West find themselves in a dilemma similar to that of the Corinthians but it does raise the more general question of how far a Christian may participate in activities of a non-Christian culture. Many feasts today are dedicated to ends so incompatible with Christianity that the question of whether a Christian is free to participate in them inevitably arises. There are activities, groups, and clubs that a strong Christian could enter but his presence there might be injurious to the faith of other Christians. The priority of the obligation of love and consideration of others, over one's own rights and liberty that Paul sets for the Corinthians, would seem to apply to a present day Christian's choice in an increasingly secularized culture.

One of the stories about St. Francis is that he and several companions obligated themselves to a fast for a long period of time. One of the members found it particularly arduous, so much so that Francis heard his brother's stomach rumbling in protest all night. Realizing it was not given to his brother to be able to endure the fast and not wishing for him to be cut off in humiliation from the group, Francis broke his own vow and ate with the brother. Francis himself was free to maintain his fast but following Paul's priorities in this passage, concerning meat sacrificial to idols, he followed not his own liberty but refrained from continuing his fast for the sake of the love of a weaker brother.

The dramatic account of the exorcism should not obscure the prior and equally important theme of Jesus' teaching. The Scripture is strangely silent about the content of that teaching. It was concerned about the kingdom and relied heavily on Scriptures, and he taught as "one that had authority, and not as the scribes." Before he is discerned to be the Messiah, the promised prophet of Deuteronomy has begun to be realized by the whole long line of prophets of Israel and completed in Christ. Both the law and the prophets function to prevent Israel from slipping into witchcraft and nature worship. St. Clement's Church in Alexandria, Virginia, has a startling entrance. On one side is a mural depicting Moses and the law and on the other side the great prophets disclosing men's inability to obey the law while both sides funnel the worshipers into the church under the arms of the cross. Here is an artistic and architectural depiction of the OT experience and its relation to the New. It illustrates the connection between our lessons from Deuteronomy and Mark.

The Fifth Sunday after Epiphany

Lutheran	Roman Catholic	Episcopal	Pres./UCC/Chr.	Methodist/COCU
Zeph. 3:14-20	Job 7:1-4, 6-7	Zeph. 3:14-20	Job 7:1-7	Job 7:1-7
1 Cor. 9:16-23	1 Cor. 9:16-19, 22-23	1 Cor. 9:16-23 22-23	1 Cor. 9:16-19,	1 Cor. 9:16-23
Mark 1:29-39	Mark 1:29-39	Mark 1:29-39	Mark 1:29-39	Mark 1:29-39

EXEGESIS

First Lesson: Zeph. 3:14-20. The prophet Zephaniah proclaimed the word of Yahweh during the reign of King Josiah (640-609 B.C.; cf. 1:1) in Jerusalem. The book is a collection of sayings; some go back to Zephaniah himself, others are later additions. The major theme emerging from the prophet's message is the Day of Yahweh. On this great and terrible day Yahweh will consume the whole earth (1:14-18; 2:2; 3:8). Zephaniah more than any other OT prophet is a man of judgment, who offers but a glimpse of the deliverance of a righteous remnant (2:3, 7). Our passage (3:14-20) comprises a late addition which may reflect a postexilic situation. It balances Zephaniah's gloomy outlook for the future: the Day of Doom is to be followed by the Day of Deliverance.

The epilogue (3:14-20) addresses Jerusalem which is to become the center of a renewed Israel. The people of the city are invited to sing an ode of joy, because the national enemy, executioner of divine judgment, will be removed. (V. 15a is phrased in the prophetic perfect; the event, though still in the future, is described as having already occurred.) Yahweh will establish himself as King amidst his people (v. 15b; cf. v. 17a). Faith in the kingship of Yahweh, while not universally popular in Israel, was closely associated with the Jerusalem temple (cf. Isaiah 6). The King's presence will dispel all anxiety (v. 15b), and Jerusalem will be called the fearless one (v. 16). No one will drop his hands and abandon his work in a gesture of despair (v. 16). The Hebrew text of the following vv. 17-18 is beset with difficulties. Part of v. 17b is best rendered with: "he will renew (you) in his love" (not: "he will be silent in love"). The full v. 17 conjures up the picture of Yahweh the warrior who shows his love in victory. V. 18b may read: "I will sweep from you the disgrace, and lift from you the reproach." The nature of the shame to be removed is specified in v. 19. The dispersion of Israel will come to an end. Those who are lame and outcast, i.e., deported, are the exiles of the Diaspora (v. 19b; cf. v 3:10). The name of Israel, held in scorn by the nations, will be exalted the world over.

Judgment is no longer the center of gravity. History inclines toward the

Day of Victory, when Yahweh the King will rally all displaced compatriots at his chosen place of Jerusalem.

Second Lesson: 1 Cor. 9:16-23. In the first part of chap. 9 (vv. 1-15) Paul speaks in defense of his apostolic freedom (cf. vv. 1a, b; 3). His custom of waiving some fundamental apostolic rights has caused some opponents to question his credibility as an apostle of Jesus Christ. Chief among the issues under scrutiny has been the right of apostles to receive material and financial aid from communities in and for which they worked. Without disputing the legality of this privilege, Paul asserts his personal freedom to abstain from it. With this decision the apostle is—according to his own words—in defiance of a command by the Lord (v. 14). The justification for his extraordinary practice of apostolic freedom is given in vv. 16-23.

He begins his plea for freedom by mentioning a "necessity" which has been imposed upon him (v. 16b). This "necessity" points to his Damascus conversion (cf. Phil. 3:12), and ultimately to his election prior to birth (cf. Gal. 1:15-16). His life as an apostle is not the result of his own free choice. Appointed in the manner of prophets (Jer. 1:5; Isa. 49:1), Paul is under a divine constraint which he cannot escape. In this sense he is a wholly unfree person. Only if he were a free man and acting on his own, could he claim earthly remunerations (v. 17a). But since he has been commissioned by God against his own will, he is like a slave deprived of all privileges. As a servant of God he has no right to ask for material rewards (v. 17b). His only personal reward is the gratifying experience of his selfless service (v. 18).

Paul's choice to forgo the right of material rewards is therefore an expression of his servitude to God. In assenting to this divine necessity, however, he gains a new freedom in his service to the people. Truly independent of any man, he can "become all things to all men" (v. 22b). He can live as a Jew with the Jews (v. 20), and act as a man freed from the law in the company of Gentiles (v. 21). Any possible misunderstandings are dispelled. His is neither a case of lapsing into legalism, nor of indulging in lawlessness. He operates from a norm which both binds and frees him.

Constrained by "the law of Christ" (v. 21) Paul strives for personal self-reliance. The freedom gained thereby allows him to serve with unreserved love. He can truly "win" the people if he speaks their language, experiences their sins, and enjoys their pleasures.

Gospel: Mark 1:29-39. Jesus' first public activity, the exorcism at Capernaum (1:21-28), is followed by an act of healing (vv. 29-31). That exorcisms and healings are a crucial aspect of Jesus' ministry is confirmed by vv. 32-34a, a Markan summary. Both activities are instrumental in implementing Jesus' major objective, the kingdom of God on earth (1:14-15).

The presence of the four disciples (v. 29) signals the importance of the healing. These same disciples will be privileged to receive Jesus' farewell speech (13:3 ff.). Peter, James, and John witness the raising of Jairus' daughter (5:21-24a, 35-43), Jesus in his transfiguration glory (9:2-8), as well as the Gethsemane agony (14:32-42). It is noteworthy that Jesus performs his first exorcism on a man and his first healing on a woman. The kingdom embraces both male and female. The significance of the healing cannot have been lost on Simon (Peter). By healing one of Simon's family, Jesus reveals his divine authority in a special way to the disciples' leader. Throughout, Simon will be both privileged by Jesus and entrusted with special responsibilities.

V. 34b is the first instance of the theology of the messianic secret. Jesus prohibits the demons to publicize his fame, not because they have the wrong conception, but because they have the right one. Silence is imposed upon them, *because* they know who Jesus is (cf. 3:11-12). Scholars are not agreed on the scope and function of the messianic secret in Mark. One obvious effect is that a veil of secrecy covers Jesus' ministry. His full identity remains hidden to men, including his disciples. It is only at the moment of his death that it dawns on the man in charge of the execution who Jesus had been (15:39).

Vv. 35-38 mark the beginning of a conflict between Jesus and his disciples. Simon and the other three "pursue" (v. 36: *katedioxen*) Jesus who had withdrawn to a place outside of Capernaum. They wish to call him back to the city of his first triumphs (v. 37). But Jesus stresses the necessity to move elsewhere so as to disseminate the message (v. 38). His mission is to cover all of Galilee (v. 39).

One might entitle our passage (1:29-39) "Jesus and Peter" (J. Schniewind). Notwithstanding Jesus' healing revelation, Simon fails to grasp Jesus' purpose. Simon seems inclined to divert Jesus from a course which is to lead beyond the city of Capernaum. While Jesus has a dynamic vision of his ministry, Simon has a more limited goal in mind.

HOMILETICAL INTERPRETATION

The passage from Zephaniah must be used by the preacher with caution. As our exegete has pointed out, the substance of the prophecy is one of judgment, a day of doom, and this is an epilogue which, if preached out of context, could be a cheap twist into a prophecy of "smooth things." Sentimentality is long range cruelty and is a besetting sin of the ecclesiastical institution. People need to be prepared for the inevitable shocks, disappointments, and tragedies concomitant with all life. Easter without Good Friday, the day of deliverance without the day of doom, deprives the worshiper of hooking his own hurt, despair, and doom to the elevating leverage of deliverance and resurrection.

The idolatry of nationalism obscures from its victim the vision of God's judgment in the action of the nation's enemy. This enemy of Israel has been the rod of God. There is enormous popular resistance in modern times to the idea of God's punishment but it is unquestionably the prophet's message that God's love includes his wrath and judgment. When a people or individual faces misfortune without considering the possibility of the prophet's message that it could be a judgment of God, they are left with the misfortune but bereft of its meaning. The defeat of the South in the war between the states is a defeat with judgment and meaning if the "national enemy," the North, can be seen as "executioner of divine judgment" (in the appropriate phrases of the exegete). Otherwise it is simply defeat. Even though this prophetic view of history does not require the instrument of God's judgment to be worthy, righteous, or better than one's own nation, still it is easy to see how the prophet's message is often regarded as unpatriotic or treacherous. However unpopular, the end result can be grace in adversity and meaning in tragedy, rather than mere adversity and mere tragedy. With a complete reliving of doom and judgment the present is combined with a foretaste of the final deliverance that brings relief, hope, serenity, and confidence.

The alternative OT reading from Job gives an opportunity for the preacher to sanction some ventilation of despair and anger in the face of innocent suffering. In important ways this is a balance to Zephaniah's prophecy from which one could falsely infer that everything that happens is the just punishment of God. On the contrary, it is the false friends alone who insist that there is some mechanical, one to one, relationship between suffering and sin, between tragedy and justice. Instead, Job can properly be presented to anyone in agony as a model for objection, protest, and anger. Heaven knows how much disguised and smoldering resentment and anger over suffering there is in any congregation but is quite likely to be underestimated by everyone. When this anger has no ventilation it will seek devious and destructive ways of expressing itself. Controlled anger is not redeemed anger. All anger needs an object and will find one. Hence, the irrational need for scapegoats in even the most sophisticated cultures. Job expresses his anger toward God, as does the psalmist, but, sadly, too few conventional Christians believe this is possible or proper. It is urgent for any congregation to be shown the simple truth that Job and the Psalms (by which this people worshiped for more than twenty centuries) allow us the opportunity to express these honest feelings of injustice and anger to

God himself. And God can take our anger so much better than our spouses, leaders, children, parents, authorities, and selves who are the scapegoats of much unconsciously projected anger that is not allowed or given appropriate release or ventilation.

The Corinthian passage gives the preacher an excellent opportunity to correct the pervasive misunderstandings of the age in regard to freedom. The popular idea of freedom is "getting what you want" and has its roots in Voltaire, Leibnitz, and the persistent Pelagianism within the church. It is a view that ignores the necessities. Lenin's view that "freedom is the recognition of necessity" is closer to the biblical view of Paul than the common assumption that one is free when his will is implemented. The latter view begs the question of "the will" and ignores the fact that many people with obvious hang-ups and in cruel bondage are choosing and getting their will's wish. The alcoholic is choosing what, when, and how much to drink but those choices are not making him free. Robert Penn Warren in his epic poem *Brother to Dragons* has a better insight than Lenin's when he observes, "For the recognition of necessity is the beginning of freedom."

Paul's ". . . . I do it apart from my own choice, I am simply discharging a trust. Then what is my pay? The satisfaction of preaching the gospel . . ." (NEB) is a view that blends freedom, necessity, and satisfaction together. The Pelagian view of freedom sees Christianity as a religion of control instead of Paul's religion of redemption. The Christian moral life is not a mere "ability not to sin," against which St. Augustine warned us, but something better, the change of our wills by being grasped and even bound as a "prisoner of the Lord" (Eph. 4:1) to the gospel. So many have a sad picture of the moral life in which we are finally able to refrain from sin, to clench our fists and teeth in a grim persistence over temptation. Instead we have something much better than mere control. We have the hope of transformation, change, redemption. The NT portrait of our Lord is certainly not one of a "teeth gritting Jesus" who was "able not to sin" but one in which he is so compelled by love that he wishes and wills to do what he must.

In this passage Paul shows the satisfaction at being grasped by the necessity of the gospel. Ernie Banks once said that if the management only knew, he'd play baseball for nothing, he loved the game so much. His enormous salary did not compel him to endure the work to earn it, but the game itself was so enticing that the love of it tied, bound him to baseball. Certainly he is more free than a person who must make himself endure his job. Similarly the gospel so claimed Paul that it was more than his will that set him free, it was being bound to the gospel. Thus he is "a free man and owns no master" (v. 19) and is able to be a servant of all.

Perhaps no text is so often quoted to deny its original meaning as "all things to all men." It is so often quoted in criticism or derision of one's having no consistent center or integrity and adjusting one's views and values to suit any condition. Paul is radically different from this. He is free to be a servant (bondman) to all for their salvation's sake. It is not helpful to tell an alcoholic, "Joe, the trouble with you is that you drink too much." One must feel as he feels, be with him where he is in order to be of any real help. It is a paradigm for being a minister (servant) to anyone. Without empathy, identification, and understanding from the position of another person's shoes no significant grace or help is possible.

Paul's view of this ministry, this servanthood in freedom, is a key to understanding in Mark the priority for teaching and preaching the kingdom even over healing the sick. Before the exorcism in the temple and the healing of Peter's mother-in-law Jesus is preaching and teaching concerning the kingdom. After he has healed many he departs to other towns to preach "for therefore came I forth." The Greek word *therapuo* ties together all three meanings of the ministry. It is translated worship, service, and health. Paul's worship is at the same time his service and satisfaction. Our service and ministry in the kingdom of God are our worship and, at the same time, our health and wholeness. Hence, the teaching and serving of the kingdom are also the healing and redeeming of the sick. Sin is bondage, service is freedom.

The Sixth Sunday after Epiphany

Lutheran	Roman Catholic	Episcopal	Pres./UCC/Chr.	Methodist/COCU
2 Kings 5:1-14	Lev. 13:1-2, 44-46	2 Kings 15:1-14	Lev. 13:1-2, 44-46	Lev. 13:1-2, 44-46
1 Cor. 10:31-11:1	1 Cor. 10:31-11:1	2 Cor. 4:16b-18	1 Cor. 10:31-11:1	1 Cor. 10:31-11:1
Mark 1:40-45	Mark 1:40-45	Mark 1:40-45	Mark 1:40-45	Mark 1:40-45

EXEGESIS

First Lesson: 2 Kings 5:1-14. Elisha, disciple and successor of Elijah, was prophet in the north of Israel during the second half of the ninth century B.C. Known as the leader of a prophetic guild (2 Kings 2:15-16), he greatly influenced the politics of Israel and foreign nations (2 Kings 8:7-15; 9:1-3). His primary function, however, was that of a miracle worker. The memory of the man and his deeds of power was preserved in prophetic circles, and ultimately incorporated into the Deuteronomic work of history (probably Deuteronomy through 2 Kings). The bulk of the Elisha tradition consists of 1 Kings 19:19-21; 2 Kings 2—9:3;

13:14-21. Nowhere in the OT are so many miracles reported within such a small space.

Our passage (2 Kings 5:1-14) reports Elisha's healing of Naaman's leprosy in the face of adverse circumstances. The healing story begins with a captive Israelite girl recommending Elisha, "the prophet who is in Samaria" (v. 3). Naaman, equipped with a letter and stately presents, travels to the king of Israel. The latter interprets the message as a provocation to war. Elisha interferes and challenges his king's suspicion. But there is still no healing in sight because Naaman refuses to comply with Elisha's instruction. Only at the prompting of his servants does Naaman condescend to obey the prophet's word. Naaman immerses himself seven times in the Jordan and emerges a cured man.

The miracle is primarily told for didactic purposes. No special interest is manifested in the miraculous. The healing is not done by a powerful word of prayer. Nor does it occur by the force of incantations, formulae, or gestures. Indeed, such a magical performance was exactly what Naaman the Syrian had expected (v. 11). Instead, Elisha is set apart from the miracle proper. This serves to direct attention to Yahweh, the source of all power. Elisha demonstrates through his miracle the superiority of Yahweh, the God of Israel (cf. v. 15).

On another plane the miracle tells the story of Naaman. The healing occurs to benefit a man who is both a foreigner and a leper. Yahweh proves his incomparability by extending help to a foreigner who would normally be considered unclean (cf. Lev. 13—14). This provocatively humanitarian aspect will be brought out in the Christian tradition. In his inaugural sermon at Nazareth Jesus mentions Naaman's healing as an example of God's movement toward the Gentiles (Luke 4:27). Elisha's miracle serves as a demonstration of Jesus' mission: it is to the Gentiles of the world.

Second Lesson: 1 Cor. 10:31—11:1. In chaps. 8-10 of 1 Corinthians Paul develops the principles of freedom and love, using the test case of meat sacrificed to idols. Our four verses summarize this discussion.

As a matter of principle, the eating of sacrificial food is permissible (v. 31; cf. 8:8; 10:25), because things are not in themselves unclean (Rom. 14:14). For the members of Christ the goods of the earth have lost their cultic and magic quality, because "the earth is the Lord's, and everything in it" (10:26; Ps. 24:1). A thoroughgoing application of the doctrine of creation (cf. also 8:6) expunges all enclaves of holiness or unholiness from the face of the earth. Paul does not base this notion of clean and unclean on a word of the Lord. This is all the more remarkable since his view comes close to that expressed in sayings and stories embraced by the

Synoptic tradition. It seems that access to such material was not available to him. In any case, Pauline ethics is not built on a *material* separation between clean and unclean.

The emancipation from the power of idols gives no pretext for rampant abuse of freedom, because the space of freedom is controlled by the application of love (v. 32). Love is guided by concern for the other person. If one eats in the company of Gentiles for whom this meal constitutes a *status confessionis* (10:27-29a), or if a weaker brother still believes in the efficacy of the meat (8:7-13), abstention ought to be practiced for the sake of the brother. What determines one's course of action is not things in and of themselves, nor personal preference, but the other person's conscience.

Love is also guided by concern for the common whole. Paul seeks "not his own advantage (*to emautou symphoron*), but that of the many" (v. 33b). What is "helpful" (*symphoron*) is what benefits the community. Paul would agree with Aristotle who considers a tyrant a man who "looks after his own profit" (Eth. Nic.: *to hauto sympheron skopei*). In Pauline ethics the profit of the individual is to be subordinated to the good of "the many" (Phil. 2:4). The ultimate good is "the church of God" (v. 32), which transcends national, social, and sexual boundaries.

Christians are entitled to "freedom from all human conventions and norms of value" (R. Bultmann). But freedom is qualified by an obligation to God and a concern for the brother. This does not mean the surrender of freedom, but its exercise in love.

Gospel: Mark 1:40-45. The Galilean ministry of Jesus is saturated with healings and exorcisms. Jesus authenticates his divine authority by deeds of superhuman power; he triumphs over sickness, mental instability, and even death. This Christology of power is not representative of the whole gospel. Jesus is also subjected to suffering and death. But the passion narrative is not to be understood in the sense that it cancels out the deeds of power (thus many interpreters, past and present). Jesus' control over the perils of human life is not invalidated by his humiliation on the cross.

There exists a close affinity between the miracle of the healing of the leper (1:40-45) and the exorcisms in Mark. The healing is described in terms of a cleansing. The leper begs Jesus to make him clean (v. 40: *katharisai*), and Jesus responds by performing a cleansing (v. 41b: *katharistheti*; v. 42: *ekatharisthe*). It seems as though the leper is a demoniac plagued by an unclean spirit (*pneuma akatharton*, cf. 1:23, 26-27; 3:11, etc.). Jesus' state of agitation also fits the nature of an exorcism. In v. 41a many commentators prefer the *lectio difficilior*: "Jesus was angered" (*orgistheis*), rather than "he was moved by pity" (*splangchnistheis*). Jesus is moved by anger because he recognizes the leprosy to be a manifestation of evil; the sick man brings him face to face with the powers of evil. V. 43 (dropped by Matthew and Luke!) fits the milieu of an exorcism. Even though the man is healed, Jesus still holds strong feelings toward him, and orders his departure similar to the way in which he casts out demons (*exebalen auton*; cf. 1:34, 39). The dramatic depiction of the story indicates a power struggle between Jesus and an evil spirit.

On a different plane the healing brings Jesus closer to a confrontation with the religious establishment. The unclean man is disqualified by society and considered a sinner before God. By letting this leper come near and touch him Jesus violates the protective laws of his religion (Lev. 13-14). The successful healing carries an indictment against the priestly establishment, if the establishment recognizes the healing, while refusing to acknowledge the person and power of the healer. (The last clause of v. 44 reads: "as testimony *against* them," cf. 6:11; 13:9.)

The manifestation of Jesus' miraculous powers is directed against the forces of evil, and puts a heavy burden on the religious authorities. Despite Jesus' effort to keep the healing hidden (v. 44b), the man cannot but make it public (v. 45).

HOMILETICAL INTERPRETATION

The story of Naaman's cure provides the preacher with an opportunity of continuing the theme of the mission imperative in Epiphany. God is not merely the God of the Israelites but it was by Naaman that "the Lord had given deliverance to Syria." Jesus uses the example of Naaman, pointing out that there were many lepers in Israel during Elisha's time but only Naaman, a Gentile, was cleansed. This example evoked wrath and attempts to kill Jesus on the part of his hearers. The anger evoked by the wider claim of God's rule versus the idolatrous attempts by fallen man to limit God's sway is an abiding tension in all times. It is no wonder that Luther could remark, "The heart of man is an idol factory." The tendency to draw one's horizons ever closer is the direction of death for individuals as well as institutions. The breaking down of walls frees those who are the victims of their own incarceration.

A theological student once spent a summer working in a parish serving native British West Indians in the Caribbean. On his return to the States he expressed doubts concerning any contribution he may have made but enormous gratitude for having his horizons widened. Citing Thomas Wolfe's *You Can't Go Home Again* he exclaimed how his home could never again be the limits and measure of his life's view. He now had a view of the world from which to see home rather than his home as a way to view the world. It is very close to the statement in the early church's

Epistle to Diognetus about a Christian's view of the world: "Every fatherland is a foreign land and every foreign land is a fatherland." The surpris-
ing grace about the Christian mission is that the giver and sender is the
inadvertant recipient of a freedom from his own incarcerating idolatries.

Mission and ministry are inseparably connected, and the story of
Naaman provides a congregation with an occasion to recall the essential
character of ministry, servanthood. As the mission imperative erases
narrow horizons, the ministry of servanthood breaks the armor of pride,
hubris. Naaman's knowledge of Elisha's power is dependent on a servant
girl. When he gets the prophet's directions he refuses to follow them
because Elisha did not seem to treat him with the dignity he deserved. His
arrogant condescension toward Israel's river prevents him from bathing in
the Jordan. It is again through servants that this "mighty man of valour" is
humbled and healed.

The relationship between humility and healing is the crucial and
decisive one. There is a bit of Naaman in each of us. In all sick marriages
and broken friendships our pride is an inevitable barrier, and it must come
down in humility for healing to take place. Humility, however, is not
claiming that you are unable to play the piano when you can. Usually false
humility is but subtle pride that seeks to shield us from exposure. Nothing
we can try to do produces humility. It is the by-product of true servanthood. When we have become committed to the service of the kingdom all
effort and accomplishment are less than the subject deserves.

When we take seriously St. Paul's injunction in the lesson from Corinthians that whatever we do we "do all for the glory of God" the duties of
our servanthood are under such demand that humility is the only possible
result. This humility, however, is not mere humiliation but a deeper
freedom. The sinful aspect of pride is the attempt to fashion such an
armor of our own dignity that we are immune from attacks, from all
charges of being wrong. To do all for the glory of God is to transfer our
dignity to this kingdom. Hence as such a servant Paul showed his freedom
from condemnation by saying, "Why am I blamed for eating food over
which I have said grace?" (NEB). This freedom is extended to all that we
do when we have in gratitude done it for God's glory. The function of
pride is replaced by dedicated service and we no longer need the armor
that more effectively separates us from love than it defends our dignity.

Mark continues the theme of cleansing the leper. It would be ill-advised
for the homily to contain much digression into dermatology. The point for
both OT and NT lessons is that leprosy to them was a symbol of sin, and
like sin it is contagious, more to be cleansed than healed. Jesus violates the
code by touching the leper but his power over unclean spirits, sickness,
and death is demonstrated by the miraculous cure. Having broken the code

he then follows the code by sending the man to show himself to the priests following the Mosaic requirements spelled out in Leviticus in the alternative OT lesson. This action of breaking and fulfilling the law at the same time is a symbolic act summing up the entire meaning of Jesus' ministry. Although he touches the leper, heals on the sabbath, and forgives sinners in violation of the law, he comes not to cancel but fulfill the law. Jesus placed before the priests the radical decision to break the code themselves in not accepting the leper's cleansing, or to accept it, thereby recognizing the power and authority of Jesus over the law.

The proclamation of Jesus as Lord should similarly place contemporary hearers in the predicament of the priests, calling them to transform their present commitment to a higher call, their present loyalty to a deeper faith. Jesus violates the very standards we live by when he breaks the code of race, group, denomination, and nation with a love that cannot be contained within the limits of any tradition.

The so-called messianic secret has the same function for a modern ear that it did in Mark's time. The miraculous power of Jesus over suffering and death cannot be denied without doing violence to both the biblical data and the continuing witness. However, Mark does not want Jesus followed for the wrong reason, because he is a miracle worker, but because of his victory on the cross. Jesus heals the leper for "He was moved by compassion." He is teaching and preaching about the kingdom of God but incidentally cannot refrain from healing those he encounters. This attracts crowds to him who are there not to discern who he is but what he can do. He tries to avoid the crowds because the claim of the kingdom is higher than the claim of being a walking hospital, even though healing is a derivation of the kingdom as well as the fruit of genuine compassion.

Only in Jesus' full disclosure of himself are human hearts transformed. The leper's disobedience of Jesus' injunction not to tell indicates that healing his skin has not changed his heart. He has not become a disciple. Where were all those countless persons who were healed by Jesus when he was betrayed, brought to trial, offered to the crowd to be released, and finally crucified? Because of his compassion he heals them. That is what *social mission* love must do. But his love seeks a deeper goal than miracles of external change, the very heart of a person must be evoked by his life, buried in his death, and raised in his discipleship.

A dermatologist of long experience once observed that his patients urgently wanted a medicine they could put on their skin to cure their disease but characteristically resisted any prescription that would change their diet or their way of life. What is true of his patients is true of congregations. We wish to have the symptoms treated and healed but resist the deeper and more radical transformation occasioned only by the cross.

The messianic secret is that the transforming faith is not that of super-human miracles but that which has been born not on the skin but in the heart on the cross. Some have attempted to preserve the secret by denying the miracles but that would seem to be a perverse way to make the secret functional. Instead it seems obvious that faith is a conjugation of many different levels of trust. Without the miracles it is doubtful that the disciples would have been brought to the deeper meaning and miracle of the cross. Likewise with us, trusting on the surface can begin a process by which successive encounters in life move us from faith to greater faith.

The Seventh Sunday after the Epiphany

Lutheran	*Roman Catholic*	*Episcopal*	*Pres./UCC/Chr.*	*Methodist/COCU*
Isa. 43:18-25	Isa. 43:18-19, 21-22, 24b-25	Isa. 43:18-19, 22, 24b-25	Isa. 43:18-25	Isa. 43:15-25
2 Cor. 1:18-22	2 Cor. 1:18-22	2 Cor. 1:18-22	2 Cor. 1:18-22	2 Cor. 1:18-22
Mark 2:1-12	Mark 2:1-12	Mark 2:1-12	Mark 2:1-12	Mark 2:1-12

EXEGESIS

First Lesson: Isa. 43:18-25. Deutero-Isaiah, the author of Isaiah 40-55, spoke the will of Yahweh to a people in exile. Aroused by the sweeping conquests of the Persian King Cyrus, he anticipated a momentous turn-about in the life of the Babylonian exiles: Cyrus, the "Lord's anointed" (Isa. 45:1), will defeat the Babylonian empire (Babylon was taken in 539 B.C.), and the expatriates will return to the Promised Land. Our passage (Isa. 43:18-25) is divided into a word of hope (vv. 18-21), a word of accusation (vv. 22-24), and a word of forgiveness (v. 25).

Of the three fundamental confessions of Israel—exodus, David, and Zion—the exodus tradition is the most prestigious in Deutero-Isaiah. Salvation equals exodus. But the exodus which lies ahead for the Israelites will prove to be an unparalleled experience. "The former things" (v. 18), e.g., the exodus of old (cf. vv. 16-17), are past and ought not to be remembered. The rescue out of Egypt belongs to a phase which was concluded with the exile. Now "a new thing," the first stirrings of which are already in the air (v. 19a), is close at hand. The exiles will return to the homeland, all things will be restored to the state of perfection (vv. 19b-21a), and the renewal will be echoed in the people's praising of Yahweh (v. 21b). The very newness of this experience dissociates Israel from her past. Deutero-Isaiah directs attention toward the future, pre-paring for an eschatological view of history.

This declaration of hope is further enhanced by the statement of accusation (vv. 22-24). Israel has brought the misfortune of exile upon herself, because she did not truly give Yahweh the honor due to him. The people had not offered their lavish sacrifices to Yahweh. The "me" of v. 22 is emphatic by position: "it was not me that you invoked, O Jacob." The prophet deplores the abuse and misdirection of the sacrifices; he does not, like Amos, denounce the cult *in toto*. Vv. 22-24 pronounce a sweeping indictment against Israel's worship of Yahweh up to the exile. Instead of serving Yahweh, the people made him their servant. V. 23b ("I did not burden you to serve me") and v. 24b ("you made me serve—with your sins") use the same word for serve, *abad*. For a moment a key concept of Deutero-Isaiah, the Servant (*ebed*) of Yahweh, comes into view. Despite Israel's guilt, the "new thing" remains valid. Yahweh's forgiveness does not depend on the worthiness of the people (v. 25).

Second Lesson: 2 Cor. 1:18-22. Paul's chief purpose in writing 2 Corinthians is to vindicate his apostolic authority and personal integrity against people who had serious misgivings about him as an apostle and as a man. The fact that he was bold on paper, but unimpressive in person, that his appearance belied his literary genius, raised the specter of deception (10:10). He was considered a coward (10:1), a mentally disturbed person (5:13), as well as an embezzler of funds marked for the Jerusalem Christians (8:20-21; 12:16-17). Our passage (1:18-22) answers to the charge of inconsistency. Due to a change in travel plans Paul did not pay the Corinthians a previously promised visit (vv. 15-16). This breach of promise further confirms the opponents' suspicion that Paul is dishonest and hence not an apostle at all.

Paul opens with a solemn formula, "God is faithful" (1 Cor. 1:9; 10:13b), which underscores the gravity of the issue (v. 18). Although Paul changed his mind on the visit, the substance of his gospel should not be affected. ("Our word to you" refers to the message of the gospel.) The sincerity of his word rests on God, the author of the word. In v. 19 the apostle further distracts from the specific charge by focusing upon Jesus, the Son of God. The full title Son of God is virtually absent in Pauline theology (Gal. 2:20; cf. also Rom. 1:4). Its use in v. 19 may be precipitated by Paul's concern to trace the gospel through Jesus back to God. As Son of God Jesus was unwavering in his obedience to the will of God. The three witnesses to the gospel may have been introduced as an additional guarantee of authenticity. V. 20a describes Jesus' affirmative role in his people's history. This history does not end in vacuity, for the questions that had remained unanswered have found their answer in Jesus (Rom. 15:8b). Beginning with v. 20b Paul's language reflects the sphere of death sentence (14:64). At an early point Jesus' manifestation of power is pitted against the Jerusalem power structure. His very display of authority as Son of man provokes the forces which will bring about his destruction.

HOMILETICAL INTERPRETATION

The prophet's declaration is threefold as our exegete points out. "The new thing" calls to mind Gal. 6:15: "Circumcision is nothing; uncircumcision is nothing; the only thing that counts is a new creation" (NEB). Circumcision was a sign of the covenant but it could not enable men to keep the covenant. Second Isaiah brings to a close the old exodus and discloses "a new thing." We are neither to remember nor consider former things. In spite of the accusation there is the promise not to remember Israel's sins. God gave the inheritance to Abraham by promise (Gal. 3:18). The Second Lesson adds: "He is the Yes pronounced upon God's promises, every one of them" (NEB). That Yes to all the promises is revealed in the Gospel lesson as one who performs miracles and forgives sins. The interrelated themes are: the new creation, the promise, the power, and the forgiveness of sins.

What makes Mark's account so difficult to grasp today is that little in contemporary times corresponds to the scribes' view that only God can forgive sins. Forgiveness of sins seems so easily available, for the price of a newspaper and the time to read an advice column. There is little sense that the law is God's and only he can forgive. In fact it was blasphemy to the scribes for Jesus to forgive sins and, as the exegete points out, it was this charge on which he was put to death. It is observed that there is "no such thing as a free lunch"; someone has to pay for it even if the recipient doesn't. For the recipient of forgiveness, like the recipient of the lunch it is not cheap but free. The cost is elsewhere, on a cross. The power of this confrontation with the scribes is lost unless the force of their high esteem for the law is appreciated.

W. B. Yeats, although not seeing himself as a Christian appreciated more the cost of saving man than many theologians.

> Odour of blood when Christ was slain
> Made all Platonic tolerance vain
> And vain all Doric discipline. [1]

If we can take "Platonic tolerance" to stand for all "sensible" restraint, acceptance, and permissiveness; and "Doric discipline" for all law and order, civilized demands, and moral imperatives; then Yeats is telling us what Paul had proclaimed in Galatians, namely, "that neither circumcision

---

1. *The Collected Poems of W. B. Yeats* (New York: MacMillan, 1956), p. 211.

There is a poignant and urgent need then to declare as a "dying man to dying men" (Richard Baxter) that "Christ is the Yes pronounced on God's promises, every one of them." John Donne said it quite well.

> One of the most convenient hieroglyphics of God is a circle; and a circle is endless. Whom God loves He loves to the end; and not only to their own end, to their death, but to His end, and His end is that He might love them still. [3]

An important minor point is the phrase "reasoning in their hearts." (The NEB's use of "mind" to translate *kardia* is unjustified.) The biblical view of man was three dimensional with his mind in his head, his feelings in his abdomen, and his reasoning center in his heart. The seventeenth century marked a movement upward with reason in the head, emotions in the heart, and the deeper instinctual feelings were orphaned. Pascal's famous quote is an example of this transition and a protest against it. "The heart has its reasons that reason doesn't know." What makes this matter of importance is that so much religious insight is dependent on a whole and total perception. Moderns are often victims of thinking themselves relegated to merely animal means of knowledge. With what organ did Jesus perceive their faith? With what organ did he see the thoughts of the scribes? It is by so many unseen human attributes that things of the spirit are known. Many realities are accessible only to caring, courage, compassion, recalling, and commitment. A congregation could be helped to see this through the example of Helen Keller who was blind and deaf from infancy yet was able to "hear" and "see" more reality than most people with their animal faculties unimpaired. With the peculiarly human faculty of a "reasoning heart" we are able to perceive and to know God in Christ, the Word in scripture, and the Body in the bread.

3. Quoted from John Baillie, *A Diary of Readings* (London: Oxford University Press, 1955) p. 284.

The Eighth Sunday after the Epiphany

Lutheran	*Roman Catholic*	*Episcopal*	*Pres./UCC/Chr.*	*Methodist/COCU*
Hos. 2:14-16 (17-18), 19-20	Hos. 2:14b, 15b, 19-20	Hos. 2:14-23	Hos. 2:14-20	Hos. 2:14-23
2 Cor. 3:1b-6	2 Cor. 3:1b-6	2 Cor. 3:17-4:2	2 Cor. 3:17-4:2	2 Cor. 3:1b-6
Mark 2:18-22	Mark 2:18-22	Mark 2:18-22	Mark 2:18-22	Mark 2:18-22

EXEGESIS

First Lesson: Hos. 2:14-16 (17-18), 19-20. Hosea is the only one of our writing prophets who was active in the Northern Kingdom. His ministry may be dated between 750 and 725 B.C. Witnessing the decline of Israel, he may not have lived to see the Assyrian conquest of Samaria in 721 B.C. He is a prophet of both judgment and hope. In this sense his theology conveys an insight basic to the OT and NT: as sin persists, so does the possibility for salvation.

The bulk of Hosea's criticism is directed against the Canaanite cult of Baal. The north was known for its syncretism. Under King Ahab and his wife Jezebel Baal worship had received strong royal backing. By Hosea's time this cult had virtually become the religion of the masses. Its appeal lay in a sensuous approach to life. Cultic prostitution and vegetation rites celebrated the victory of life and fertility over death and sterility. Hosea, although utterly opposed to the cult, nevertheless uses images of love and metaphors of nature which betray his indebtedness to the prevailing Baal milieu of his day.

As a lover woos his girl, so does Yahweh lure his people into the desert for deliverance (v. 14). Even though there once was "trouble" in the desert, now it is the place of hope. (In the Valley of Achor, i.e., Valley of "Trouble," Achan was stoned for stealing forbidden spoils; his guilt brought "trouble" upon Israel; cf. Josh. 7:22-26.) Despite the incident in the Valley of "Trouble," the wilderness stay is considered Israel's ideal time. Then and there the relationship between Yahweh and his people had been uncorrupted by false lovers. This ideal time will now be restored. The salvation to come is a return to the past (v. 15a). Out of the wilderness a new creation will arise. Yahweh's bride, i.e., Israel, will once again be to her bridegroom what she had been "in the days of her youth" (v. 15b). The adulterous relationship with the Baals is to be replaced by the kind of love a wife shows toward her husband (vv. 16-17). The marriage will be sealed in a covenant of peace (v. 18). All hostilities between man and beast, and man and man will be terminated (cf. Isa. 11:6-9; 2:4). Nature and history are to be reconciled. Yahweh offers his bridal gifts of righteousness, justice, love, and mercy (v. 19). Israel in turn will "know" Yahweh with the intimacy that exists between a woman and a man (cf. Gen. 4:1).

Second Lesson: 2 Cor. 3:1b-6. In a widely acclaimed study on Paul's opponents in 2 Corinthians, D. Georgi succeeded in illuminating certain aspects of Pauline theology. In 2 Corinthians Paul contended against Jewish-Christian missionaries who were primarily engaged in prophetic interpretation of Scripture, pneumatic ecstasy, and the performance of miracles. These missionaries considered themselves endowed with divine energy, and they saw their main function in the display of signs and wonders. When Paul characterizes these opponents as "super apostles" (11:5; 12:11), he refers to their manifestations of power. In broad historical perspective, these "super apostles" were representatives of a prevalent religious mode of expression, the Hellenistic Divine-Man (*theios aner*) ideology.

The Divine-Man missionaries had arrived at Corinth equipped with letters of recommendation, written no doubt by influential Christians of other communities. These documents in all probability were epistolary summaries detailing the missionaries' apostolic virtues and spiritual accomplishments. Paul criticizes his opponents (v. 1b) for adopting the conventional practice of using such reference letters. (Paul himself, however, wrote a letter of recommendation—to Philemon on behalf of Onesimus.) His own letter of recommendation is the people of the Corinthian church (v. 2; cf. 1 Cor. 9:2b). The very existence of this church is indelibly written on the heart of Paul; at the same time the church's existence is for all the world to see (v. 2). While the opponents, despite their spiritual exhibitionism, rely on the force of ink and paper, Paul's "letter from Christ" is written with the abiding quality of the living Spirit (v. 3). Paul's living letter is superior even to the Mosaic tablets at Sinai (v. 3). The people themselves form the basis of Paul's apostolic confidence, a confidence "through Christ toward God" (v. 4). No further credentials are needed. The opponents are likely to have mistaken their personal appearance in power for the source of all power. Paul reminds the Divine-Man apostles that there is no such thing as religious self-sufficiency (cf. 2:16b); his and their power are from God (v. 5).

Paul argues that the very ones who preach and practice the supremacy of the Spirit are crucially dependent on certificates of paper. It is implied that the opponents still serve under the Old Covenant (v. 6). This is Pauline polemic which should not be understood in the historical sense that the missionaries were Judaizing representatives of the Jerusalem church (Tübingen thesis!). Paul's point is that the opponents still live spiritually under the Mosaic code, because they have failed to grasp the Spirit of the New Covenant.

Gospel: Mark 2:18-22. This fasting pericope reflects a complex process of transmission and interpretation. It is immediately obvious that the final version resulted in a reversal of the story's earlier, and possibly original intention. Initially, the disciples' nonobservance of fasting is set in contrast with the fasting practice of John's disciples and the Pharisees (v. 18). In direct response to this situation Jesus sanctions his disciples' total non-compliance with the fasting regulations (v. 19a). Vv. 19b-20, however, assume a time when fasting had become a fact of Christian life. Now the Christian observance of fasting is justified.

The difference between the two versions on fasting is due to Jesus' presence and absence respectively. During the lifetime of Jesus his movement in part claimed independence by violating the practice of fasting which had been sacred to both John and the Pharisees. Many scholars regard v. 19a as an authentic Jesus saying (cf. J. Jeremias, N. Perrin). The presence of Jesus proved to be incompatible with the traditional days of fasting. The eschatological novelty of his mission forced the break with Judaism and the movement of John. Vv. 19b-20, however, appear in the form of an amendment which is designed to deal with changing conditions. It is safe to assume that this latest version makes contact with the Markan situation. The death of Jesus brought about a reconsideration of earlier practices. Now complete freedom from fasting has lost its appeal for Mark, and one day is officially assigned for fasting. "On that day" (emphatic by position) specifies the preceding reference to the days of Jesus' violent removal, and points to Good Friday. In its present form, the pericope serves to endorse Friday as the day of weekly fasting.

The Christians' resumption of fasting after the death of Jesus does not, however, denote a return to Judaism. The day of crucifixion has provided the stimulus for a reconsideration of time. If during Jesus' lifetime the disciples were at variance with Judaism by their nonobservance of fasting, after Jesus' death the Christians' fasting on Friday contrasts with the Jewish fasting on Monday and Thursday.

The amended version of the fasting pericope continues the eschatological thrust of Jesus' ministry. This is expressly stated in the sayings collection (vv. 21-22) concerning new patches on old garments, and new wine in old wineskins. No compromise is allowed between the new and the old. The new life of the kingdom is gained at the price of breaking loose from the traditional order of life.

HOMILETICAL INTERPRETATION

Hosea's situation in the eighth century B.C. is much closer to ours than one would first expect. Baal worship was essentially an attempt to resolve the problem of being human by means of the powers of nature, particularly fertility power. Within the history of Christianity there has been a tendency to combat the seduction of nature worship and the danger to community latent in sex by going to otherworldly extremes. K. S. Latourette points out that most of the world-denying heresies condemned by the early church found their way back into Christianity via monasticism; as a result traditional ascetic practices have molded to a great extent the mind of modern men concerning the content of the Christian faith. Hence, the prevailing assumption today concerning flesh versus spirit is a far cry from its OT and NT significance.

At the same time our culture has become religiously preoccupied with sex. The lesson from Hosea offers the preacher an opportunity to disclose this deeper religious dimension to what is often regarded as merely a moral problem. As one does not need be a Fascist to be against Communism, or vice versa, so the preacher must be careful not so to oppose one error as to appear to condone its opposite. Hosea provides a golden opportunity for a modern person to see the exceedingly dangerous tug of nature worship in unhooking us from our fidelity and commitment to the righteous God of history.

Such people as Norman O. Brown urge modern man in a direction comparable to Baalism in the OT. In his ending of *Love's Body* he proclaims a new garden, a new Eden, where there "will be no one to answer to." If there is no God and Father to call to account the sons of Adam, Brown argues, then there is no guilt and we are freed from all the neurotic results of guilt (which Christianity has called sin), while at the same time there is enough at the breast of Mother Nature for everybody. It is a utopian vision that accounts for sin and evil, not in man and a fallen nature (often not so much a mother as a stepmother) but in man's being held accountable by a God of history. Norman O. Brown seems to offer an elimination of sin and evil by eliminating accountability. There is an accelerating growth in modern groups reflecting in varying degrees just such spiritually seductive aspects reminiscent of Baal worship.

At the same time Hosea's example helps us avoid the opposite error in any flight away from history or any identification of nature and sex with evil. On the contrary, what is wrong with such things as prostitution is not that they are dirty but that they are unfaithful. Hosea does not hesitate to use the language of romance and sex as illustrations of our relationship with Yahweh. There is a strange blend of Victorianism and Freudianism that giggles or gives sly grins at the sexual analogies of God's relationship with his people. C. S. Lewis' chapter on "Eros" in *The Four Loves* is an excellent source for treating this subject with the proper appreciation of the goodness but demonic inadequacy of *eros*. The eighteenth century poet, Christopher Smart, expresses this aspect of Christianity:

> God all-bounteous, all creative,
> Whom no ills from good dissuade,
> Is incarnate, and a native
> Of the very world he made.[1]

This incarnational theme is carried on in the Corinthian lesson. Paul contrasts the external credentials of his critics' letters of recommendation with those of his converts whose changed lives are his credential letters, written not with ink but on the "fleshy tables of the heart." His being beset by detractors, claiming the authority of the Spirit, is especially relevant to our times. There are a growing number of similarly conflicting claims in many churches and this rule of thumb could equally apply today: "By their fruits ye shall know them" and the true Spirit writes on the "fleshy tables of the human heart." The charismatic movement today is a combination of great grace mixed with sin and manipulation (most frequently unconscious). Paul's way of dealing with conflicting authorities is to put them to the incarnational test: which authority redeems, transforms, loves, and brings more life and light?

An even wider application is the contrast Paul makes between fleshy tablets (community of people) and stone tablets (Mosaic code), between the spirit of the law and the letter of the law. In the academic and professional world institutions are threatened by an exclusive reliance on external credentials—Ph.D.'s, professional diplomas, and accrediting standards—and need always to be drawn back to the reason for their existence: the student, the patient, the client, and the parishioner. Are their credentials written on the transformed hearts of their charges, or are they merely etched on paper behind glass hanging on a wall?

The issue of fasting treated by Mark has had something of a similar history to that of sex. Because fertility cults abused religion in their affirmation of sex, so in reaction the church has tended to undervalue sex. Similarly, because fasting has been abused in the church in negative and legalistic ways, the reaction has been to undervalue fasting altogether. As our exegete points out, the church's resumption of fasting must not entail a return to Judaism. To fast on Friday rather than on Monday and Thursday could be to fall back to an old legalism and lose the new dimension of freedom given to Christians.

1. *The Hymnal* (New York: Oxford University Press, 1940), no. 320.

Traditional functions for fasting have been to keep the body in subjection, to express repentance, to influence the action of God, and help relive portions of Christ's life. Jesus himself fasted but he explicitly dissociated his mission from the fasting traditions of John and Judaism. The Christian dimension to fasting similarly must offer fasting to a congregation on a level of freedom inaccessible to legalistic traditions and the world.

Christ's victory over sin and death enables a Christian to fast as a celebration, a celebration of independence. "Man does not live by bread alone" and Christians need to be reminded of the victory that has set them free from the powers of this world. A body needs food to survive but fasting is not starvation. Fasting declares the Christian's sure and certain hope that the end of this body is not the end of man. Our citizenship is in heaven against which the gates of hell shall not prevail. As we set aside a time to recall our independence as a country, we set aside a time to fast to celebrate our independence, to declare our freedom in Christ.

The Transfiguration of Our Lord
The Last Sunday after Epiphany

Lutheran	Roman Catholic	Episcopal	Pres./UCC/Chr.	Methodist/COCU
2 Kings 2:1-12a	Dan. 7:9-10, 13-14	1 Kings 19:4-12	Dan. 7:13-14	2 Kings 2:1-12a
2 Cor. 3:12-4:2	1 Peter 1:16-19	2 Cor. 4:3-6	Rev. 1:4-8	2 Cor. 4:3-6
Mark 9:2-9	Mark 9:1-9	Mark 9:2-9	John 18:33-37	Mark 9:2-9

EXEGESIS

First Lesson: 2 Kings 2:1-12a. Our passage is a prophetic succession story which sanctions the transfer of power from Elijah to Elisha. It is as much a story of Elijah and his mysterious departure, as it is of Elisha and his singleness of purpose.

The setting of the story is Elijah's last journey, which is a journey, not unto death, but to the ascension (cf. v. 1 with Luke 9:51). Accompanied by his disciple Elisha, Elijah travels from Gilgal to Bethel and from there to Jericho and across the Jordan. Three times along the way Elijah asks his companion to let him proceed alone (vv. 2a, 4a, 6a), but each time Elisha declares with a solemn oath that he will not leave his master (vv. 2b, 4b, 6b). At Bethel and Jericho guilds of prophets remind Elisha of the journey's end and purpose (vv. 3, 5). The possible implication of their reminder is to talk Elisha out of following Elijah, because Elijah's departure was to be a mystery, not witnessed by anyone. But Elisha asks the prophets to remain silent, and continues his journey with Elijah. As they reach the Jordan, Elijah reproduces Moses' miracle of the cleaving of waters (v. 8; cf. Exod. 14:16, 21-22), whereupon the two cross through the river on dry ground. This feat is witnessed by fifty prophets from the distance (v. 7). On the other side of the Jordan Elijah permits his persistent companion one last request, and Elisha asks for a "double share" of Elijah's spirit (v. 9). This request is based on the law concerning the first-born (Deut. 21:17), and it reveals Elisha's determination to become the principal successor to Elijah. In his response Elijah leaves the gratification of his disciple's desire to the divine will; Elisha must be found worthy of the sight of Elijah's mysterious ascension (v. 10). Instantaneously Elisha witnesses his master's triumphal procession in a fiery storm (v. 11). As eyewitness to the translation, Elisha is finally qualified to bear the mantle of Elijah.

Elisha is rewarded with the crucial sight of Elijah's glorification because he has traveled his master's road to the end. The journey has served him as preparation for his succession to Elijah. Elijah's mysterious translation in the wilderness east of the Jordan has inspired the concept of his return in Jewish and Christian tradition alike. Under the impact of apocalypticism Elijah is assigned the role of eschatological precursor (cf. Mal. 4:5). The Synoptic tradition identifies him with John the Baptist who may have ministered in the general area of the ascension scene (cf. John 1:28)!

Second Lesson: 2 Cor. 3:12—4:2. Our passage is a Midrash on Exod. 34:29-35, directed against the opponents of Paul. Recent investigations into the nature of the opposition theology in 2 Corinthians (S. Schulz, D. Georgi) allow us to follow Paul's argument more accurately than was hitherto possible.

Paul's opponents in 2 Corinthians are Jewish—Christian missionaries who hold the Torah and Moses in high esteem. According to their understanding of Exod. 34:29-35, Moses had put a veil over his face because the people would not have been able to bear the sight of it. "The skin of Moses' face shone" because he had gained direct insight into the Sinai mystery. The missionaries consider themselves, and only themselves, to be in possession of the Spirit. This permits them, like Moses, to perceive the glory of Sinai so that their bodies and faces reflect the presence of God.

Against these missionaries Paul argues that Moses had used the veil to prevent the Israelites from realizing that the glory reflected on his face was fading. The Mosaic veil illustrates the deficient nature of the glory. It had not been a protective device, but a means of deception, used to cover up the incompleteness of the old covenant (vv. 12-13). With this argument Paul disavows his opponents' primary source of revelation, i.e., Moses and the Sinai tradition. The veil which had concealed the face of Moses still lies upon the hearts of the people (vv. 14-15). The reference to "heart" (v. 15: "a veil lies upon their heart," not "minds") polemicizes against the opponents' claim to physical manifestations of power. Even if they glory outwardly, inwardly they have remained imperceptive and unredeemed (cf. 5:12). Only in Christ is the veil of incomprehension removed and the truth in Scripture perceived (v. 16). The difficult v. 17 is an argument against the missionaries' definition of their spirit alone as the Spirit of God. Paul breaks their exclusive claim to the Spirit by identifying it with the Lord, i.e., Jesus. As a result of the freedom won in Christ all people (v. 18: "and all of us"), not just the few, reflect as in a mirror the glory of the Lord. One does not, however, possess the presence of Christ as an ontological substance, rather one grows into it in a process of transformation (v. 18).

Paul dismisses his opponents' commitment to Moses and the Old Covenant, because this position betrays a superficial and exclusive understanding of Christ.

Gospel: Mark 9:2-9. The transfiguration scene is located on a mountain; of the mountains mentioned in the Gospel (3:13; 6:46; 13:3), it is the only "high mountain" (v. 2). Towering above all other peaks of revelation, the "high mountain" ascended by Jesus and his three confidants designates the transfiguration as the epiphany of all epiphanies. The transformed status of Jesus is described by the whiteness of his garments (v. 3). White, the color of the end time (cf. Rev. 6:2; 7:9; 14:14), imparts an eschatological quality to the transfigured Jesus. The Jesus the disciples are privileged to witness is Christ in his final, future glory. Both Moses and Elijah figured prominently in Jewish and Christian expectations of the end time. Their joint appearance on the "high mountain" further underscores the eschatological character of the transfiguration epiphany (v. 4). The cloud is the traditional manifestation of the presence of God (cf. Exod. 24:16), and the voice coming out of the cloud is none other than the voice of God (v. 7a). This heavenly voice marks the only direct intervention of God in the ministry of Jesus—outside of baptism. At Jesus' beginning God had in a similar way and with nearly identical words taken the initiative (cf. 1:11 with 9:7). At baptism Jesus, the Son of God, was installed into the office of the eschatological king. But the installation ceremony was shrouded in secrecy; nobody witnessed the eschatological irruption of the Spirit, not even the Baptist himself. With the transfiguration the disciples are informed of Jesus' future installation as the Son of God. The transfiguration, closely modeled after baptism, anticipates Jesus' coming in apocalyptic fullness, i.e., his parousia.

Unlike all other epiphanies in the gospel, the transfiguration is provided with the date of its final disclosure (v. 9). It is to remain under cover until the resurrection of the Son of man. The resurrected Jesus is thus not identical with the Jesus of the transfiguration. Rather, the resurrection marks the *terminus post quem* of the realization of Jesus' transfiguration glory. The transfiguration points outside itself into the post-resurrectional life of Christ—to his parousia in glory.

Throughout the Gospel of Mark the disciples fail to understand Jesus. The transfiguration is no exception. In a state of fear and confusion Peter suggests the building of three booths (vv. 5-6). His idea is motivated by the compulsion to seize upon what was only meant to be a prolepsis of the future. Peter mistakes the future for the present.

HOMILETICAL INTERPRETATION

The transfiguration offers the preacher several themes on which to concentrate. It is certainly the eschatological way to view the present and it gives to the present its transforming hope (cf. 2 Corinthians 12: "Seeing then we have such hope"). In Mark's account the disciples could not understand this event until after the passion and resurrection. For us, this side of Easter, the transfiguration is a renewed opportunity to look at our present situation in the light of its future and purpose and thereby to redeem it. W. P. DuBose in his *Soteriology of the New Testament* insisted that no definition is complete without including its purpose (or its final cause). It is not enough to say what a thing *is*. One must go on to say what it *is for*, what it was to be, its intention and destiny. This is true of everything from a monkey wrench to a person. One would not think of explaining to a child what a pipe wrench *is* without saying what it is *for*. But unfortunately we often assume the identity of a person merely on the basis of his *is* without including also his purpose and end, what he is *for*.

One quite moving illustration of the transforming power of the trans-figuration way of discerning the present is in the figure of Don Quixote in *Man of La Mancha*. This comic figure tenaciously refuses to let the "is" take final precedence over "what will be." He insists on calling, naming, wording, regarding Aldonza the Whore as "My Lady Dulcinea." This wording from the eschatological perspective of her destiny, end, and purpose begins to transform Aldonza. Near the end of the play Don Quixote is dead and his comrade Sancho Panza speaks to Aldonza. She replies to him in a quiet but powerful serenity, "My name is Dulcinea."

It was from the mountain top of the transfiguration that Martin Luther King, Jr. found his inspiration and vision for that great speech in Washing-ton, D.C. "I've been to the mountain top . . ." His vision was not the vision of what had been, nor what is now, but of what is to be. This vision of the end and destiny of things applies not only to people and situations, redeeming them, but also to suffering.

Scholars of Mark's Gospel have argued that the purpose of the secret here is to lay emphasis not merely upon the power of the Son manifested in miracles but upon the suffering of the Son manifested in his passion. The mystery of suffering is an ambitious subject for any sermon but the transformation by the transfiguration should be an important part of any approach. For many years the most requested copy of all sermons preached on "The Protestant Hour" was one on suffering by the Rev. John Redhead. There can be no question of the widespread need for attention to this subject. In whatever way God is, or is not, involved in the cause of suffering, all can agree in all cases that he is Lord over all suffering. In Rom. 8:18 Paul connects the glory of the transfiguration with the way we are enabled to regard any suffering now. "For I reckon that the sufferings of this present time are not worthy to be compared with the glory which shall be revealed in us" (Rom. 8:18).

This glory is common to the three lessons. For Paul the ministration of Moses was glorious but not to be compared with the glory of Christ's new covenant. The veil that was over Moses' face hides the limitations of the law's glory. Even now, the veil over the hearts of his adversaries hides from them the new more glorious service. Paul's contention against the Judaizers in Galatians and against the more subtle distorters in Corinth, continues down through the history of the church into our own times. John Wesley, after his conversion, wrote a blistering letter to William Law complaining that the latter had never told him of this new and more glorious ministration. One has but to read some traditional devotional writings, looking in vain for any declaration of acquittal, forgiveness, and justification, to realize that there yet persists those whose hearts are veiled with the old law and are strangers to the freedom of this righteousness. (cf. 2 Cor. 3:17)

V. 12 of the Second Lesson begins with an important assumption, "Having therefore such hope . . .," that must not be overlooked. It comes as a great surprise to many church people that the opposite of "condemnation" is "righteousness!" "For if the service of condemnation be glory, much more doth the service of righteousness exceed in glory" (v. 9). The word "righteousness" here is the same as justification, and the doctrine of justification has been interpreted in recent times as mere "acceptance" or as a permissiveness inconsistent with this biblical term "righteousness." On the other hand, in each age and in each congregation, there remain hearts veiled from the knowledge of this righteousness which is the opposite of condemnation.

We then are moving from the condemnation of the old service to the righteousness and freedom of the new service. The key word for Paul seems to be "glory" as it appears in v. 18. It is the glory that comes to us from beholding the glory of the Lord, and our identity moves "from glory to glory" by the Spirit of the Lord. There is a lie taught by the world that our glory comes from within ourselves. It was the advice of Polonius to Laertes in *Hamlet*, "to thine own self be true," and is correctly diagnosed as the pull of death in the contemporary musical comedy *Pippin*, "But I've got to be me." Both themes beg the question of who Laertes and Pippin really are. Paul is telling us that neither they nor we know who we are except in the service of him who is the expressed image of both God and our eschatological identity, our true intention, destiny and purpose. Hence the word "service" (*diakanos*) should not be obscured by the King James "ministration" nor by the NEB "dispensation" (v. 9).

When Elijah replies to Elisha that he will be granted what he asks if Elisha sees the departure, the transfer of power is left to the divine will. It is a foretaste of the request by the disciples of Jesus to sit on the right and left side and of Jesus' reply that this was not his to give but was related to their willingness to drink of the cup that he drank of (Mark 10:38). Elisha's persistence, as a follower of Elijah's ministry, is the occasion of his receiving the latter's power. Similarly, the disciples' persistence in following the way of Jesus was the occasion of their empowering. Likewise today, our doing God's service is the occasion of our glory (as his grace and word are its cause).

Peter, missing the true meaning of the transfigured Christ, wishes to make tabernacles to memorialize the event rather than see it as a way to view all events. Like Peter the ecclesiastical institution is always tempted to freeze and memorialize the vision rather than transform events by the power of its hope.